Tai Magic

TAI MAGIC

Susan Conway

Silkworm Books

ISBN 978-616-215-215-3

Second edition published in 2025 by
Silkworm Books
430/58 M. 7, T. Mae Hia, Chiang Mai 50100, Thailand
info@silkwormbooks.com
https://silkwormbooks.com

Typeset in Minion Pro 11 pt. by Silk Type

Printed and bound in Thailand by O. S. Printing House, Bangkok

5 4 3 2 1

Contents

Illustrations

Introduction

This book is a study of a Tai magico-religious belief system practised in the Shan States in Myanmar and in Lan Na in northern Thailand. The fieldwork for the book took place between 2009 and 2013 and the research in the UK and USA over a longer period.

Chapter 1 analyses the Tai belief system, which comprises five elements: Theravada Buddhism, a belief in spirits, the power of nature, healing, sacred objects, astrology, Buddhist cosmology and numerology. The text indicates how this belief system is illustrated in diagrams and illustrations on mulberry paper and cloth.

Chapter 2 examines the arts of the supernatural using illustrations from mulberry paper manuscripts. It examines where inspiration for these illustrations came from. Did it come solely from the spirit world, inspired by dreams and hallucinations, or were tangible images sourced from this world? The author suggests sources for expressing what good and evil spirits look like and how they can inspire a sense of awe, fear, desire, love or repulsion. Examples are given of individual spirits and how an image (*yantra*), a combination of magical illustrations, diagrams and texts, transferred onto mulberry paper or cotton is translated into positive or negative power. Methods and materials used for drawing and painting images are given.

Chapter 3 introduces Pali incantations and magic spells (*katha*) used with *yantra*. It explores the process of using the time a person was born, the position of the planets and the phases of the moon in calculating how an individual is treated. The author notes the variety of Tai, Burmese and

Khmer script used in *yantra* diagrams and gives examples of how texts can be reduced to letters, phrases and numbers in code or formulated to represent phonic spells. Examples are given of how *yantra* and *katha* are used in specific rituals.

Chapter 4 focuses on painted and printed textiles that bring to life cosmological landscapes and the good and evil spirits that inhabit them. It reveals how characters from the spirit world can transition to the world of humans. In terms of imagery, the author selects the mandala as an expression of the basic principles of Buddhism and the spirit world. Regional variations in style and proficiency are noted. Examples of individual spirits and their attributes are given. The chapter then focuses on divination textiles and includes predictions on when to build and when to fight wars. The final section explains the power of talismanic textiles for many forms of protection.

Chapter 5 moves to the present and explores how *yantra* and *katha* and accompanying rituals have been reworked to suit current physical and mental health needs. It includes the treatment of refugees and migrants who have fled over the border from Myanmar into Thailand. The focus is on monks, lay *saya* and herbalists whose work is healing, divination, creating good luck and minimising bad luck among the local population and recent arrivals. The author interviewed monks, lay *saya* and herbalists in Mae Hong Son and Chiang Rai and in the Shan State of Keng Tung, noting differences in modern treatments with those from the past. The use of herbal remedies with medical treatment by doctors was an interesting discovery.

Chapter 6 presents the historic art of tattooing, an essential part of the Tai magico-religious belief system. Tattoos ward off evil spirits, protect the body against sickness and injury and have the power to create popularity. They bring respect from others, success in love and can be activated to make a person invisible. The process in passing from an apprenticeship to becoming a tattoo master is explained with the rituals involved in preparing a client for a tattooing session.

An explanation of the equipment and tattooing process is given, along with accounts by the author of the tattooists she interviewed in the Shan States in Myanmar and northern Thailand. Descriptions of tattoo images are provided from tattooing manuscripts belonging to the men interviewed and from museum collections in the USA and UK. The chapter ends with a plea for conservation and protection of Tai tattoo manuscripts as important records of the past to be accessed for research and education. The author highlights the problem of antique dealers scouring poor villages for manuscripts that they break up to sell to private collectors or to interior decorators as 'primitive' art.

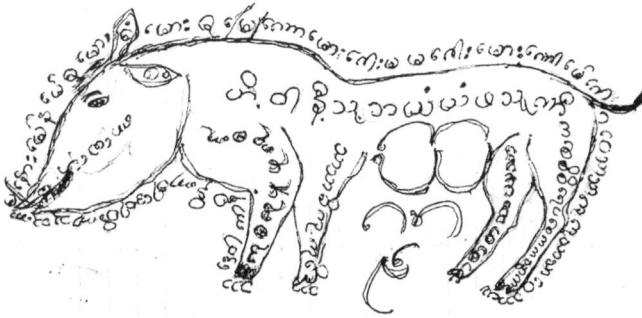

A *yantra* of a wild pig, copied in a notebook from a Shan manuscript,
Wat Pang Mu, Mae Hong Son.

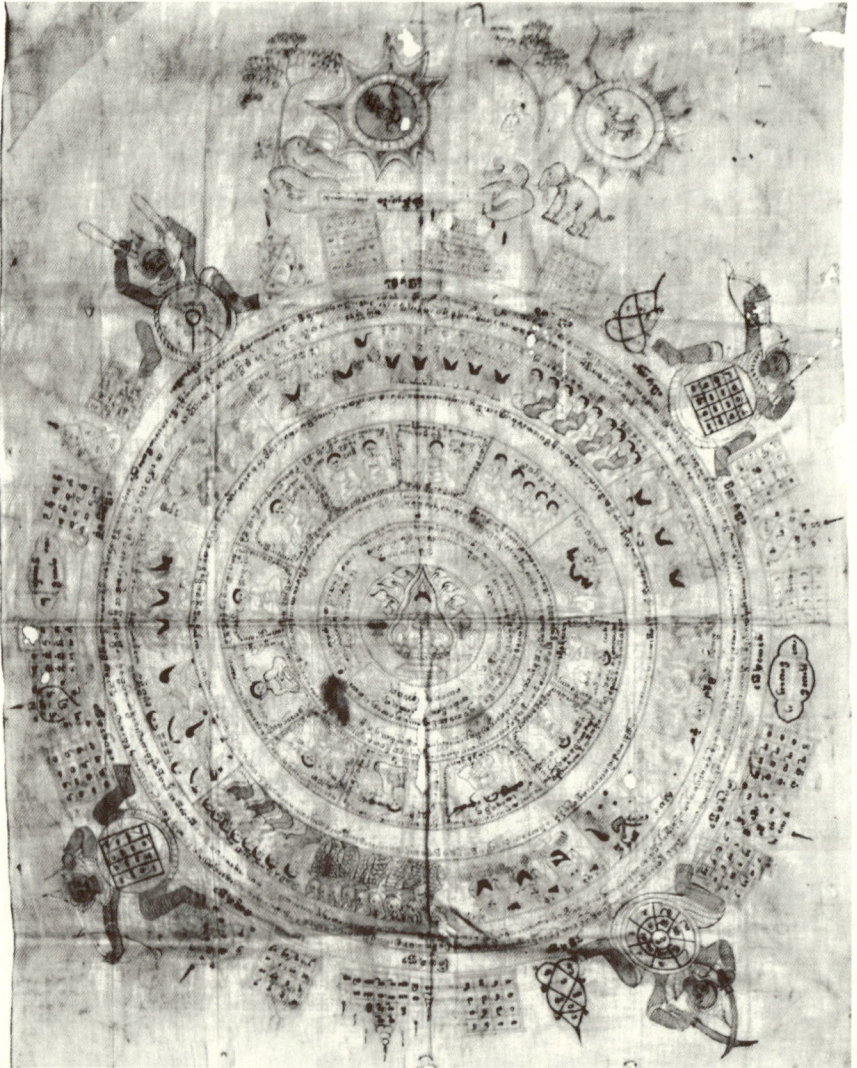

A cotton printed and painted mandala for protection and meditation, Shan style (de Siam Antiques).

CHAPTER 1

SETTING THE SCENE: ELEMENTS OF THE TAI BELIEF SYSTEM

People who perform magic are summoning supernatural forces that interact with the paranormal. In simple terms, they are calling good or bad spirits. The Tai of Shan State (Tai Yai) and the Tai of Lan Na (Tai Yuan) call this *saiyasart*. Those who perform *saiyasart* for good purposes are called *saya* or *zaray*. This broadly means a craftsperson or artisan. Those who use *saiyasart* for evil purposes are called *maw paeng*. The terms 'shaman' and 'witch doctor' are purposely avoided here because they lack flexibility to define a system that involves Buddhist monk practitioners and laymen and women.

Evidence of supernatural practice is found in all major religions. This chapter introduces the belief system that underpins Tai supernaturalism. Tais believe in the power of Theravada Buddhism (doctrine and practice), spirits (good and evil spirits), healing, sacred objects, the force of nature, astrology, Buddhist cosmology and numerology.[1] These beliefs have evolved with traces of Siamese, Hindu and Chinese culture. Monks and *saya* gain power and prestige as keepers of the system and as followers of established precepts.

The Tai respect the power of spirits. Every family has a spirit house in the garden or a communal one if they live in apartments. Spirits live in the vicinity of monasteries, farms, commercial properties and government buildings. Urban and rural people, rich and poor make offerings at spirit

---

1. Analysis provided in Thai by the Ven. Phrakhru Vimol Silpakit of Mahachulalongkorn-rajavidyalaya University, Wat Phra Kaew. Translated by museologist Rebecca Weldon Sithiwong, Chiang Rai, December 2011.

shrines. Many have protective talismans in their cars and amulets on the handlebars of their motorbikes, a form of protection reinforced with a blessing from a Buddhist monk. A university-educated government officer taking up a new post consults a *saya* versed in astrology and divination to predict his future. A poor migrant labourer seeking work will do the same if he can afford it. Both hope to secure good luck and protect against bad luck.[2] In the language of insurance brokers, they are managing risk and immeasurable uncertainty.[3]

Summoning supernatural force involves calling and appeasing the spirits with the aid of *yantra*, a combination of magical illustrations, diagrams and texts. Manuscripts provide practitioners who prescribe *yantra* with the necessary information, including Pali incantations and magic spells (*katha*), chanted to accompany *yantra*. Some *saya* specialise in herbal medicines and ointments as part of treatment, and there are manuscripts dealing specifically with herbal remedies. Before countrywide education, *saya* unable to read and write learnt this information by rote. *Saya* use *yantra* to generate positive power and neutralise negative power. *Maw paeng*, in contrast, make prescriptions using polluted substances and herbs to deal with evil spirits, ghosts and witches. All practitioners have faced the problem of gathering herbs when the wholesale destruction of forests has diminished supplies.

Most *saya* practising in villages and small towns know their clients although they tend to keep themselves apart from everyday village life. Wives and relatives, on the other hand, are acquainted with their neighbours, for example if there is illness in a family or money worries. This is useful information for a *saya* asked to help and where female members of the

2. Governments and travel companies put focus on ancient rituals as a way of promoting tourism and the 'exoticism' of the East.

3. Frank H. Knight, Risk, *Uncertainty and Profit*, Boston: Houghton Mifflin, 1921; quoted at the ANRC and RCSD Workshop on 'Human Security and Religious Certainty in Southeast Asia', Chiang Mai, Thailand, 15–17 January 2010.

family can assist in preparing appropriate ritual materials. Monk *saya* are familiar with village communities because they are regular attendees at the monastery, helping prepare for celebrations as well as providing a regular presence on holy days. In present times, as people have moved away from rural communities into cities, these bonds have become strained or entirely broken. In contrast, *maw paeng* are strictly private figures and operate covertly because of their association with evil practices. Villagers say everyone knows someone to go to but they are not prepared to identify who the person is. I was told that in the city of Keng Tung in Shan State there was only one active *maw paeng*.

The eight elements of the Tai belief system as given to me are explored below.

1. Theravada Buddhism

Theravada Buddhism is the major religion of the Tai of Shan State and Lan Na. Monasteries are situated in every community and are a focus for an annual cycle of Buddhist rituals. Until the era of state education, monasteries provided education for boys. This was an opportunity not available to girls, with a few exceptions among the elite and girls taught by Christian missionaries. Not all boys were educated as they could not be spared from farms, nor were they able to become novices, as was common among young men. However, they developed practical ways to pay tribute to the Buddha, for example by carving Buddha images from medicinal wood and offering them to a monastery.[4] Males who could be spared were inducted as novice monks during the Lenten period of three months. Most then returned to their villages although some stayed to become fully ordained. Men could enter the monastery later in life, perhaps towards the end of a career, bringing useful experience to the religious community. There were also monks making the opposite transition by returning to a lay community

---

4. Chiang Rai Museum has a collection of these images.

as respected elders. Movement between religious and secular life meant a constant interchange of ideas and practices between monastery and village. This exchange included farming experience and knowledge of herbal medicines as villagers kept herb gardens and went into local forests to gather ingredients. Some monasteries had herbal manuscripts in their libraries that monks used for prescriptions and to learn the chants and spells needed to activate them.

Monks who practise healing today are charismatic figures who attract many followers. Their source of power is self-discipline and restraint, achieved through strict observance of up to and beyond two hundred Buddhist precepts. The longer a monk is ordained, the more he radiates *metta*, the Pali term for loving-kindness, benevolence and harmony. It is a state devoid of self-interest, devoted to bringing benefit to others, in Pali, *parahita parasukha kamana*. Just the presence of a monk with these attributes brings goodness and negates the power of malevolent spirits.

Two elements of the belief system come together in the language of rituals. Pali, a Buddhist language, is used with colloquial languages. In the 1960s the anthropologist and Lan Na scholar Kraisri Nimmanahaeminda described a guardian spirit ritual held outside the city of Chiang Mai. Chanting in Pali was, for those present, a form of protection and a way to banish unruly spirits that craved human flesh.[5] Colloquial language, on the other hand, was a way to appease the spirits. Over twenty years later, Sommai Premchit and Amphay Doré witnessed a ceremony in which a *saya* invoked the spirits and spoke on their behalf in a local language while a monk used Pali language for incantations intended to limit any negative power the spirits might

5. Kraisri Nimmanahaeminda, 'The Lawa Guardian Spirits of Chiangmai', *Journal of the Siam Society*, 1967, 55(2): 185–225.

generate.[6] The choice of language itself thus contributes to balancing and controlling power.

If spirits are uncontrolled and causing chaos, the beneficial power of monks is vital in the process of restoring order. Wild spirits are blamed for hooliganism, disrespect and bad behaviour, particularly among young men, including drunkenness, profanity and violence. Exorcism involves monks chanting in Pali and displaying images of the Buddha during the chanting.[7] The relationship between unruly spirits and the orderly world of Buddhism is represented in some manuscript illustrations. A well-known monster spirit with ogre-like features, armed with knives, looks capable of coming to life and jumping off the page but will not do so because he is constrained within a circle of Buddhist text.

Theravada Buddhism is a religion with a conformist following, but there is room for *saiyasart*, often referred to as 'not strictly Buddhist'. Tattooing falls into this category, although monk tattooers are becoming a rarity as commercial tattoo parlours take over. Most tattoo artists are lay *saya* but there are monks, often latecomers to the monkhood, who practised before being ordained. As monks they are restricted to tattooing iconography that generates beneficial power. However, the process of tattooing involves calling and appeasing the spirits. This anomaly is dealt with by allocating space where tattooing is practised to the back area of the monastery grounds, away from the main monastic complex where Buddhist rituals are held. The building contains an altar where clients make offerings to the spirits before being tattooed.

Although they live apart, monks are not remote from the communities they serve. The monastery is often the place where valued manuscripts, like

6. Sommai Premchit and Amphay Doré, 'The Lan Na Twelve-month Traditions: An Ethno-historic and Comparative Approach', Research Report, Faculty of Social Sciences, Chiang Mai University, Thailand, and Centre National de la Recherche Scientifique, France, 1991, pp. 249–53.

7. Kraisri, 'The Lawa Guardian Spirits of Chiangmai', pp. 185–225.

the ones referred to in this book, are entrusted. Charismatic monks and *saya* develop reputations and attract followers from long distances who come seeking advice and treatment.

2. The Power of Spirits

A spirit is a mystical, supernatural entity that can possess humans, animals and natural objects. Some are evil spirits that appear as ghosts and witches. Spirits are pacified on a regular basis. If disturbed or offended in some way, a spirit may leave the space it normally occupies. Living beings are susceptible to loss, particularly when physically vulnerable, for example newborn babies, young children and pregnant women. Farm animals are at risk in periods of hard labour, such as pulling ploughs before rice planting and heavy-laden carts at harvest time. If a spirit leaves its normal dwelling place, a ritual is organised to call it back. The exception is at the time of death when spirits accompany the body to another world.

The repetitive chanting of "Please come" specifically addresses lost spirits, but there are many longer incantations for calling and also *saya* skilled at calling in the tradition of Tai poetry reading that involves special rhythmic patterns and intonations. People admire the rising and falling cadence of these chants, and appreciation is said to extend to the spirits who listen and are more likely to respond.

Spirits exist in a hierarchy established in parallel with hierarchies of the earlier inhabitants of the land. The Tai were migrants who settled in small numbers among existing Lawa inhabitants, whose spirits they acknowledged. The Tai were diligent in appeasing Lawa spirits, fearing drought, famine, floods and disease if they did not do so. The Lawa erected stone and wooden pillars to appease guardian spirits and Lawa chiefs presided over animal sacrifice and spirit possession rituals.[8] The Tai were Buddhist but practised

---

8. Eric Seidenfaden, 'The Lawa: An Additional Note,' *Journal of the Siam Society*, 1923, 27(3): 101–2.

similar spirit rituals with *saya* officiating. By the thirteenth century CE, the Tai outnumbered the Lawa, and their spirits became dominant although they continued to acknowledge Lawa spirits. Ruling Tai families invited Lawa chiefs to attend court rituals to bring good luck.[9] This was an enduring custom that continued until the Tai princely states were dissolved and power moved from Shan State to Burma (Myanmar) and from Lan Na to Siam.[10]

Tai ancestor myths tell of royal spirits descending from Heaven on jewelled ladders to take human form. Shan and Lan Na Tai rulers were addressed as "Lord of Life". They were mediators between guardian spirits and the people and conducted rituals to appease powerful guardian spirits at major city shrines. They presided at rain-making ceremonies to ensure successful crop yields and went on pilgrimage to other spirit shrines. They funded the production of large rockets fired during fertility rites. Their role as mediator between the spirits and the people ended when the princes lost power – the Shan to central government in Burma (Myanmar) and the Lan Na princes to the court in Bangkok. Regionally appointed governors and military officials took control, presiding over rituals that had previously been the responsibility of Tai royalty.

In contrast to royalty, common people were born from giant gourds, and they interact with lesser spirits. The language used to address spirits was hierarchical, as royal spirits were addressed in polite court language whereas colloquial language was used in addressing lesser spirits. This hierarchy is evident in the architecture and design of spirit shrines. The senior guardian spirit of a Tai state (*phi chao mueang*) warrants a grand spirit shrine. He has

9. Ratanapanna Thera, *The Jinakalamalipakarana Chronicle* (The Sheaf of Garlands of the Epochs of the Conqueror), Mss, Rattavanavihara Temple, Chiang Mai 1516 CE; trans. N. A. Jayawickrama; reprinted London: The Pali Text Society Translation Series 36, 1968.

10. Susan Conway, *Silken Threads Lacquer Thrones: Lan Na Court Textiles*, Bangkok: River Books, 2002.

jurisdiction over spirits that protect monasteries.[11] He controls the spirits of villages and towns occupying less grand spirit houses. Each household has its own spirits that dwell in a spirit house in the garden where food is offered daily. Spirits dwelling in the fields, on footpaths and along animal tracks are acknowledged in humble shrines usually made from local wood and bamboo. Spirits living in the forests, hills and mountains are left offerings at the base of ancient trees and rock formations.

Evil spirits are harbingers of bad luck, vengeful, malevolent and discordant. Ghosts are disembodied humans who, because of evils committed in previous lives, are reborn to haunt the living. They are blamed for many forms of mental illness. An exorcist is needed to deal with them. Witches are malicious human beings who act out of hatred and spite either on their own volition or on behalf of clients. Witches are careful to hide their identity from those around them and their work is highly secretive.

Experts who perform spirit rituals undertake an apprenticeship, usually set up through family networks. A man without family connections must find a *saya* willing to take him on. An apprenticeship can last up to ten years. Part of the training involves wearing white robes, learning *yantra* and *katha* and when to administer them, and for some how to prepare herbal remedies. Specific rules govern the lives of *saya*. They include dietary restrictions, including refraining from eating offal and animal intestines, leftover food and dishes prepared for consumption at funeral rites.[12] Other rules are based

---

11. The positioning of a monastic spirit house is an ecclesiastical decision. See Stanley Jeyaraja Tambiah, *Buddhism and the Spirit Cults in North-east Thailand*, Cambridge: Cambridge University Press, 1970.

12. Interview with Gaysorn and Kan-na (Sua Yen) Rubnamtham, Mae Hong Son, January 2010. They settled in Mae Hong Son Province from Shan State.

on Buddhist precepts, except for chastity. A *saya* can marry. The more rules a *saya* obeys, the more power he gains to communicate with the spirits.[13]

The power of a *saya* is enhanced by physical endurance, particularly the painful process of tattooing. A *saya* may be extensively tattooed. There are men who, to increase their power, have endured the process repeatedly until their skin is black except for their face, the palms of their hands and the soles of their feet.[14] Old age adds to power, and a *saya* claiming to be at least a hundred years old is not uncommon. Ownership of ritual materials gives added authority, particularly manuscripts passed down through a lineage of *saya*. They mark a man apart from other villagers.

Saya practise at home with a separate area in the house for meeting clients. Some maintain a separate building. There is an altar (*khan khru*) with candles, images of gods and goddesses, manuscripts and astrological charts, cleansed with holy water at New Year. Clients come carrying offerings for the spirits, such as flowers, fruit, betel, beeswax candles and milled and unmilled rice. They first have a consultation and a fee is agreed. There are a variety of requests. On a social level, clients want help to make friends and increase their personal standing in society. Businessmen come for good luck in commercial ventures and harmony between business partners. Some ask for longevity and protection against injury. Others seek luck in love. The sick come for healing although they can be visited at home if too ill to travel. The rituals *saya* perform deal with physical and mental illness. Today most go to doctors for conventional medical treatment but may also consult a *saya*.

On a countrywide scale, a *saya* may be asked to appease the spirits following apocalyptical events like floods, drought and disease epidemics.

---

13. The Five Precepts are no killing of a living object, no stealing, no falsehoods, no adultery and no consumption of alcohol. The Eight Precepts add to the Five Precepts three other restrictions: no food after noon, no entertainment unless of a prescribed moral nature and living without comfort by sitting on the floor during the day and sleeping on the floor at night.

14. A ritual expert was tattooed thirty-seven times. Interview with Maha Kaew, Keng Tung, 2007.

In 2011 a flood destroyed crops across large areas of agricultural land in the valleys of Lan Na, leading to major appeasement rituals. A disastrous plane crash led to similar appeasement rituals in Chiang Mai. In the present conflict in Myanmar, Shan soldiers go to *saya* for protection against injury and death in battle.

Monks and *saya* administer supernatural formulae (*yantra*) on mulberry paper, although there are records of leaves and wood being used.[15] Each prescription is matched to a client's birth data and associated planetary force, a system explained later in this book. The time to administer a *yantra* is calculated according to auspicious time periods. There is chanting and a series of breath exhalations held over the *yantra*. Instructions are given on when and how to perform the ritual. A *yantra* can be prepared with a time delay before it becomes potent, usually up to a week. This is beneficial when a member of the family is tasked with carrying it back to a sick relative some distance away.

Monks and *saya* negotiate with spirits to generate positive power whereas *maw paeng* deal with evil spirits that create negative power. They are secretive figures who operate in the shadows, their work a taboo subject. To hire a *maw paeng* involves a contract and an agreed price. A time and day are set by consulting astrological charts.[16] *Maw paeng* operate in cemeteries, at the site of freshly dug graves and on derelict land. They acquire by dubious means or steal funeral cloths, animal and human bones and cremation ash. They take shavings from wooden poles used to turn corpses on funeral pyres and add polluted water, human and animal excrement, hairs from suspect witches and disease-carrying insects to their concoctions. Stealing or secretly acquiring profane ingredients, particularly from cemeteries, is repugnant but enhances the evil power of the thief, with covert operations taking place in the cover of darkness.

---

15. Susan Conway, *Tai Magic: Arts of the Supernatural*, Bangkok: River Books, 2014.
16. Interview with Gaysorn and Kan-na Rubnamtham, Mae Hong Son, January 2010.

Maw paeng magically introduce polluted substances into the bodies of victims and cast evil spells on them. The negative power they create brings physical and mental illness, and in extreme circumstances, death. Businesses go bankrupt, children fail exams, guilty verdicts are pronounced on the innocent, the healthy unexpectedly fall sick. But creating negative power comes with a caveat. Those of strong moral character who live honest lives as devout Buddhists and observe at least five Buddhist precepts should not be victimised. If a *maw paeng* successfully targets an innocent victim, this evil power can be reversed by a powerful *saya* who observes many precepts. The more power the evil spirits generate, the more precepts the *saya* must follow to reverse it. If he is not successful, a Buddhist monk is asked to intercede. However, there is a code that operates according to *karma*, bad actions in previous lives that decide fate in this life. Those who live blameless lives in this life cycle may not escape being targeted by a *maw paeng* because they committed serious offences in a previous life.

People who deserve to suffer are those who cause serious physical and mental harm to others, damage or destroy property on at least three occasions and disrupt harmony in society. Practising in such an environment can be risky even for a *maw paeng*. Evil spirits responsible for aggressive behaviour are difficult to control. They possess men who become drunk and disorderly, harass monks during Buddhist ceremonies and desecrate graves. Many are mentally unstable. Evil spirits can turn against the *saya* trying to control them. If that happens, he recites powerful Pali incantations praising the Attributes of the Buddha, the Eightfold Path and the Triple Gem. If this does not achieve the desired effect, he seeks help from an exorcist or from a monk whose source of power comes from self-discipline and strict observance of many Buddhist precepts.

3. Healing

This is a practice where women play an important role as herbalists. Healing remedies contain plants raised in home and monastery gardens and, in the past, gathered in local forests now destroyed by logging and mineral extraction. Herbs are harvested in home gardens or purchased in local markets. Gathering and preparing herbs takes place on auspicious days set according to a lunar calendar. Ingredients require pounding, grinding, shredding and infusing in liquid or oil. The treatments described here come from a Shan manuscript, circa 1800, in the collections of the Horniman Museum, London.[17]

Before forests were devastated, wild deer, rhinoceroses, bears, tigers, pangolins, porcupines and pythons were abundant. They were hunted for their skins, horns, teeth and internal organs. Powdered deer horn kept the kidneys and spleen healthy, strengthened bones and muscles and promoted blood flow.[18] Powdered rhino horn treated fevers and relieved the symptoms of arthritis and gout and cured headaches, hallucinations, high blood pressure, typhoid, snakebite, food poisoning and possession by spirits.[19] Bear bile reduced fever, healed inflammation and eased pain and was used to treat liver disease, haemorrhoids, heat convulsions and epilepsy. Ground tiger bone healed ulcers and burns and cured typhoid, malaria, dysentery and rheumatism. Tiger whiskers and teeth were worn as talismans to protect against all types of illnesss. Pangolin scales were dried and roasted to treat malaria and deafness, nervous conditions and women possessed by evil spirits. Porcupine bezoar, a stony secretion extracted from the stomach of a procupine, was a cure for digestive disorders and dengue fever. Python bones, gall bladder and skin treated rheumatism, headache and diabetes as well as undiagnosed ailments caused by evil spirits. Stick lac, a secretion of insects, treated liver damage, while wild honey was used for healing wounds.

17. Susan Conway, *Tai Herbalism*, Chiang Mai: Silkworm Books, 2024.

18. Chen L.; Wang X.; and Huang B., 'The Genus Hippocampus: A Review on Traditional Medicinal Uses, Chemical Constituents and Pharmacological Properties', *Journal of Ethnopharmacology*, 2015, 162: 104–11.

19. The claim that rhino horn is effective as an aphrodisiac is contested. See Jeremy Hsu, 'The Hard Truth about the Rhino Horn "Aphrodisiac" Market', *Scientific American*, 5 April 2017.

The ash from burnt ant nests was applied to skin lesions. Alum crystals, ground to a powder, treated open wounds and sores, and grass that grew over termite nests treated fungal and bacterial infections.[20]

The prescriptions described above were administered with healing rituals which involved chanting in Pali, magic spells in colloquial dialect and meditation. One of the most popular healing rituals still practised today involves hollow wax candles with texts rolled up inside. They are described as *kha-tha thon-pis*, meaning 'sacred words to withdraw negative power'. This is where knowledge of astrology and cosmology becomes important. To establish the sacred words to be used, the year, month and birthday of each client is required. This also establishes the auspicious time to light the candles.

A client who has been to a hospital or consulted a Western-trained doctor and has not been cured, may choose to seek help from a *saya*. The *saya* may diagnose possession by evil spirits, although this diagnosis is disputed. Some *saya* claim spirits are not to blame for the condition of those who suffer from chronic or inherited diseases or are physically disabled. Their disabilities are the result of *karma*.[21] Others do not accept this and claim *karma* is not responsible. Disability and chronic diseases are caused by evil spirits that target individuals, and exorcism is the correct treatment.

4. The Power of Nature

Men interact with nature to improve their chance of survival. During the transitional Bronze to Iron Age period (900–600 BCE), cave dwellers carved images of wild animals and used them as offerings to the spirits to ensure success in hunting. Recent models resemble these early carvings, such as the gilded and lacquered illustrations of bulls, bears, and other animals, resemble

---

20. Rob Verpoorte, 'Food and Medicine: Old Traditions, Novel Opportunities', *Journal of Ethnopharmacology*, 2015, 11: 29 (editorial).

21. Escape from *karma* and the endless cycle of suffering involves attaining *nirvana*, a state of enlightenment when individual human desires and suffering are extinguished.

these early cravings. They are talismans, carried while travelling, particularly through forests where wild animals and tropical disease flourished. If the carrier was attacked by a wild animal, he stroked the talisman and chanted a magic spell that brought the animal to life, full size, to protect him.[22] Elderly villagers living along the Thailand-Burma border remember their fathers carrying similar talismans when they went into the forest to hunt.[23] Others recall male relatives with protective tattoos that served a similar purpose. Stroking an animal tattoo while uttering a magic spell summoned the power of the animal. A tiger tattoo imparted bravery, stealth and speed in attack. A tattoo of a wild pig with a thick skin provided protection against knife, spear and sword wounds and the tearing claws of bears.

Today there is continuing belief that ingredients collected from the wild have more power. In 2012 there were at least six stalls in the morning market in Keng Tung selling pure beeswax, seed pods of *sompoy* (*Acacia rugata Merr.*), sheets of handmade mulberry paper and spools of local cotton thread for ritual use. Pure beeswax, used to make ritual candles, has a fragrance that attracts beneficial spirits. It burns without leaving a residue. The seeds of *sompoy* are ingredients for soap used in cleansing rituals. Handmade mulberry paper is favoured over commercial paper for candle rituals because it burns slowly, allowing time for ritual chanting. Handspun cotton is preferred for candle wicks used in healing rituals because the ply of each strand can be customised to individual clients and their birth data.

In contrast to healing through herbs and animal extracts, *maw paeng* use the destructive force of nature. They collect shavings from the bark of trees struck by lightning and scrapings from the horns and skins of animals also hit by lightning. They gain great power from human bones taken from those who die in accidents or natural disasters or are murder victims. A

22. Information provided by villagers in Mae Hong Son, January 2009.

23. Superstition about wild animal parts has not ended. Hunting wild animals is officially banned but their parts are obtained illegally.

spirit released from the body of someone who dies in violent circumstances becomes a sadistic wandering force that a *maw paeng* can harness to cause sickness and death to others.

Faith in the power of nature remains one of the principles of the Tai belief system although wild animals and forests that nurtured them have disappeared in most of Shan State. Activists against further destruction use Buddhism and spirit rites to draw attention to the issue. They call for the protection of trees and make offerings to the spirits that live in them and perform symbolic ordination services to turn trees into sacred objects, hoping to prevent more felling.

5. Sacred Objects

A sacred object is defined as an object connected to a higher being, for example the Buddha or other religious leaders like Jesus Christ. Sacred objects are considered worthy of veneration, like a Buddha image or a statue of a saint. There is a certain hierarchy in sacredness. In the Buddhist belief system, it passes down by association to monk's robes which are imbued with positive power for protection and healing. Sacredness continues after death as robes become beneficial talismans (see Chapter 4). Other sacred objects relevant to this book include statues of gods and goddesses and Pali texts. In the Tai belief system, nature is a higher being, so sacred objects include lotus flowers and ancient trees.

6. – 7. Astrology and Cosmology

At the nineteenth-century Shan and Lan Na courts, men often referred to as 'brahmins' practised divination to aid decisions taken by those who ruled. These men were not brahmins in the true Indian sense of the word but local men familiar with aspects of astrology and cosmology.[24] They prepared

24. Reginald Le May said they were not true Brahmins in the Indian sense. See *An Asian Arcady: The Land and Peoples of Northern Siam*, 1926; reprint Bangkok: White Lotus, 1986, p. 12.

personal horoscopes for Lan Na and Shan rulers and newly born princes and calculated auspicious times to conduct affairs of state and negotiate with foreign powers. They prepared complex astrological and cosmological drawings in manuscripts. This was a world away from village divination systems.

Villagers tend not to consult a *saya* if they need simple guidance, such as an auspicious time to plant rice and later to harvest it, or a favourable time to purchase farm animals. Instead, they buy Tai astrological charts in the market and make their own calculations. The moon has long been a singular tool for reckoning because it is easily visible from earth and its appearance changes every day as it waxes and wanes. The moon is portrayed as a hare pulled across the sky in a horse-drawn chariot carved with a peacock's head and tail. The time of full moon is the most auspicious and generates maximum positive power. People go to the river to draw water for its potent cleansing properties, and herbs are collected for medicine at that time. Tattoo artists favour the full moon of November as tattoos created on that night are imbued with extra force. Auspiciousness is also calculated according to the days of the week. Sunday is the day of the rice goddess Mae Posop and thus an inauspicious day to collect rice from the rice barn without offending her.[25] Monday is an auspicious day for travel. Wednesday and Friday are inauspicious for conducting cremation rituals but auspicious for calling spirits and for ritual bathing. Thursday is a lucky day for financial deals. Friday is an all-round auspicious day. These calculations serve well for events in everyday life. However, for life-changing episodes, such as being ordained, getting married or building a new house, it is appropriate to seek the advice of a *saya*. A Lan Na and Shan system for calculating auspicious and inauspicious times is built on an eight-time period system which is explained in Chapter 3.

25. The spirit of rice is Mae Khwan Khao. She ensures successful harvests. She is represented in the dress of a celestial maiden either in ethnic style or according to historical court fashion. When not represented figuratively, Mae Khwan Khao is symbolised by a ripening rice plant.

Although the eight-time period system is the most used, there is another system based on the Chinese Twelve-Year Animal Cycle.[26] In the Tai version, the Lord Buddha summoned all the animals to an audience before his final departure from earth. Twelve species answered his call. They were, in order of appearance, the Rat, the Ox, the Tiger, the Hare, the Dragon, the Snake, the Horse, the Goat, the Monkey, the Cockerel, the Dog and the Pig. As a reward for their obedience, the Buddha named one year after each of them, thus creating a Twelve-Year cycle.[27] Designated planets, gods and goddesses, the base elements earth, fire, water, iron, wood and gold, and auspicious plants are matched with each animal. In simple terms, the year you are born determines the animal and set of designations that affect your life.

Officers in Tai armies had military charts drawn up by astrologers so they could plan battle strategies, a custom recorded in thirteenth-century Tai chronicles. Astrological charts were prepared on cotton cloth after which a live chicken or lizard was placed on the edge of the cloth while its movements across the cloth were carefully scrutinised. Tactics for fighting the enemy were drawn up based on these random movements.[28] The cloths had magical protective properties and were set on fire and the ash deposit collected, diluted in water and administered to soldiers as a drink. Sometimes the ash was mixed with oil and rubbed into the skin as a body shield.[29] Incantations for victory were chanted when potions were administered.

26. The Twelve-Year Animal Cycle is mentioned in eleventh- and twelfth-century Cambodian inscriptions.

27. The system matches individuals born in a particular year of the cycle with a Buddhist temple. For example, in Chiang Mai those born in the Year of the Rat are associated with Wat That Sri Chom Thong.

28. David K. Wyatt and Aroonrut Wickienkeeo, trans., The Chiang Mai Chronicle, Chiang Mai: Silkworm Books, 1995, pp. 31–36.

29. This type of cloth is in the collections of Wat Pa Daed, Chiang Mai.

8. Numerology

A belief in the supernatural power of numbers inspires both figurative and abstract images in manuscripts and on cloth. They represent the Buddha, his followers and good and evil spirits. The process of creating images involves an auspicious number of pen marks or brush strokes made while chanting. For example, a Buddha image created with nine strokes of a brush is a popular image for meditation.[30] The first stroke represents the first virtue, the Buddha is beyond all suffering. The second symbolises the second virtue, the Buddha is the worthy one. Stroke three, the Buddha is flawlessly self-enlightened. Stroke four, the Buddha is imbued with perfect knowledge. Stroke five, the Buddha knows all worlds. Stroke six, the Buddha is without equal. Stroke seven, the Buddha is a great leader. Stroke eight, the Buddha is teacher of gods and humans. Stoke nine symbolises the Buddha is the Blessed One.

The nine-stroke Buddha has another purpose at it also symbolises the nine sacred objects of Buddhism. The first stroke is Mount Meru, centre of the physical, metaphysical and spiritual universe of Buddhism. The second stroke is the sun and moon. The third stroke denotes the *Tripitika*, the Pali canon. The fourth is the four islands surrounding Mount Meru. The fifth represents the five Dhyani Buddhas.[31] The sixth stroke, the six halos of the Buddha, and the seventh, the *Buzin Sutta*, a Buddhist text. Stroke eight denotes the Noble Eightfold Path that Buddhists follow to attain *nirvana*, and stroke nine symbolises all nine virtues of the Buddha.

Numerology is also used to calculate the number of times an incantation is repeated during a ritual. If chanted three times it symbolises the Triple Gem, the Buddha, his teaching and his community of disciples. Four times symbolises the Four Noble Truths, the importance of understanding

---

30. Melford E. Spiro, *Burmese Supernaturalism: A Study in the Explanation and Reduction of Suffering*, New Jersey: Prentice-Hall, 1967, p. 176.

31. Representing the five qualities of the Buddha.

suffering, the origins of suffering, the cessation of suffering and the path to *nirvana*. Eight times signifies the eight celestial bodies, the Sun, Moon, Mars, Mercury, Jupiter, Venus, Saturn and Rahu, and represents the Eightfold Path of Buddhism. An incantation repeated forty times signifies the forty significant stanzas of the *Metta Sutta*. Numerology is also applied in choosing materials for candle rituals. A candle with a wick made up of thirty-eight fine strands of cotton represents the thirty-eight meritorious acts of the Buddha. Fifty-six strands symbolise fifty-six virtues of the Triple Gem, and ninety-six strands the ninety-six forms of evil conquered by the power of Buddhism. The relationship between ritual objects and significant numbers is further explored in later chapters.

Yantra, Raw Materials and Power

The power associated with *yantra* is attributed to the value of natural raw materials. Paper for manuscripts and for making individual *yantra* comes from mulberry tree bark (*Broussonetia papyrifera*). The process involves cutting the bark into thin strips, boiling it in a solution of water and wood ash and pounding it with wooden mallets to create a smooth paste which is then poured onto mesh screens and left to dry in the sun. The resulting paper is peeled off the mesh, trimmed and burnished with a stone. It is generally left in its natural off-white colour.[32] In terms of ritual, the value of handmade mulberry paper is that it smoulders slowly when lit, allowing enough time for accompanying rituals to be completed.

Two types of mulberry paper manuscript were used for recording supernatural formulae. The oldest form functions like a regular sketch book or flipchart (*pap kien*). The paper is trimmed to an average of thirty by fifty centimetres, stacked, glued together along the top edge and reinforced with

---

32. Folios can be coated with black lacquer. The writing and drawings are made with white chalk and soapstone.

stitching using waxed cotton thread.[33] The size of the paper and square shape means that each page is illustrated like a regular book. The second type of manuscript (*pap tup*) has narrow rectangular sheets folded backwards and forwards in concertina-style pleats (*leporello*). The rectangular narrow shape restricts the format.

Black ink used for drawing and writing was made from fireplace soot mixed with animal or fish bile or gum from a wild plant called *ya muk*.[34] In the past, bear and monkey bile was a common ingredient. There was an alternative in commercial Chinese block ink. It was not highly rated among *saya* because ink made locally was chanted over to charge the ingredients with power.[35] When the ink faded, it was written over and recharged with power. *Saya* often added comments in the margins of manuscripts they used regularly. They noted the efficacious power of a particular spirit, the effectiveness of individual incantations and additions or modifications to potions.

Manuscripts were passed from one generation of *saya* to the next unless there was no relative to take over, then an apprentice from outside the family might be trained. Manuscripts generally survived through several generations, but if a manuscript was in a very poor condition, it would be copied and the original burnt at the owner's cremation. Or it might be donated to a monastery where it was ritually cleansed before being accepted. New copies were validated by invoking the power of the *saya* who owned the original and a celebrated ancestor *saya* whose name was passed down from one generation to the next.[36]

---

33. Front and back covers were made from several glued sheets of paper and given a coating of lacquer.

34. Information provided by the monks of Wat Pa Daed, Chiang Mai, 2009.

35. The power of the 'eighty-thousand rishis' is quoted as one source of power (see Chapter 2).

36. Interview with Gaysorn and Kan-na Rubnamtham who told me that their celebrated ancestor was called by the honorary title 'Maha Jing', Mae Hong Son, January 2010.

Textiles

The process of empowering textiles is the same as for *yantra*. The artist calls on the spirits for inspiration and chants during the creative process, the timing of the work set according to a lunar calendar. There is no work carried out during inauspicious periods. Painted and printed cloths on cotton are produced for meditation, protection and divination and for funeral rites. They vary in size from painted banners displayed during Buddhist and spirit rituals to small talismans the size of handkerchiefs. The iconography is primarily Buddhist with reference to Buddhist cosmology. Mount Meru is portrayed with an ocean of water creatures and plants. This world is inhabited by mythological humans and animals and gods and goddesses. Time is set according to an eight-time period system with images of animals, planets and stars.

But creating fantastic images is not the only method for empowering cloth. Plain cloth gains power by close physical proximity to a charismatic individual, such as a revered abbot.[37] The faithful leave objects in the vicinity in the belief that beneficial power can be transmitted to them. Monks' robes are themselves charged with beneficial power. This power is not associated only with the living. After he dies, a monk's robes are divided among the faithful. They become protective backings for wall hangings and banners and are cut and sewn as lining for talismanic vests, shirts and jackets. Fragments line hats and ritual bags used by *saya*. Small pieces become talismans carried in pockets and wallets. Funeral cloths that covered a monk's body and face at his funeral have similar power. Removed before cremation rites, they are ritually cleansed and distributed among followers. Some are taken to *saya* who add astrological diagrams, birth data and *gatha* as a way of personalising the protective power of the cloth.

---

37. The level of protection provided by these textiles relates to the status of the individual.

A Unique Art Form

There is a long tradition of creating tangible figures of spirits as part of *yantra*. Although described as scribes, it is possible to argue that these are artists providing us with imaginative renditions of what spirits look like. The flourish of a brush stroke brings individuality to the process, but this type of drawing is also a conventional religious act that suppresses the ego. Artists work within parameters that involve chanting and manipulating letters of the alphabet by elongating and compressing them into animal and human shapes. They communicate to the onlooker individual physical characteristics associated with spirits, their facial expressions and body gestures often contorted and exaggerated. The most disturbing images portray evil spirits as belligerent ogres, symbols of evil, insanity, violence and revenge. They share some characteristics with the creatures of hell painted by European artists.[38]

---

38. Like the hell scenes of Hieronymous Bosch, late fifteenth to early sixteenth century.

A painted and printed cotton cloth showing Phra Upakut who transitions from a princely spirit living in the waters under the earth to become a young monk. Eight lizards, symbols of good luck, appear between the figures.

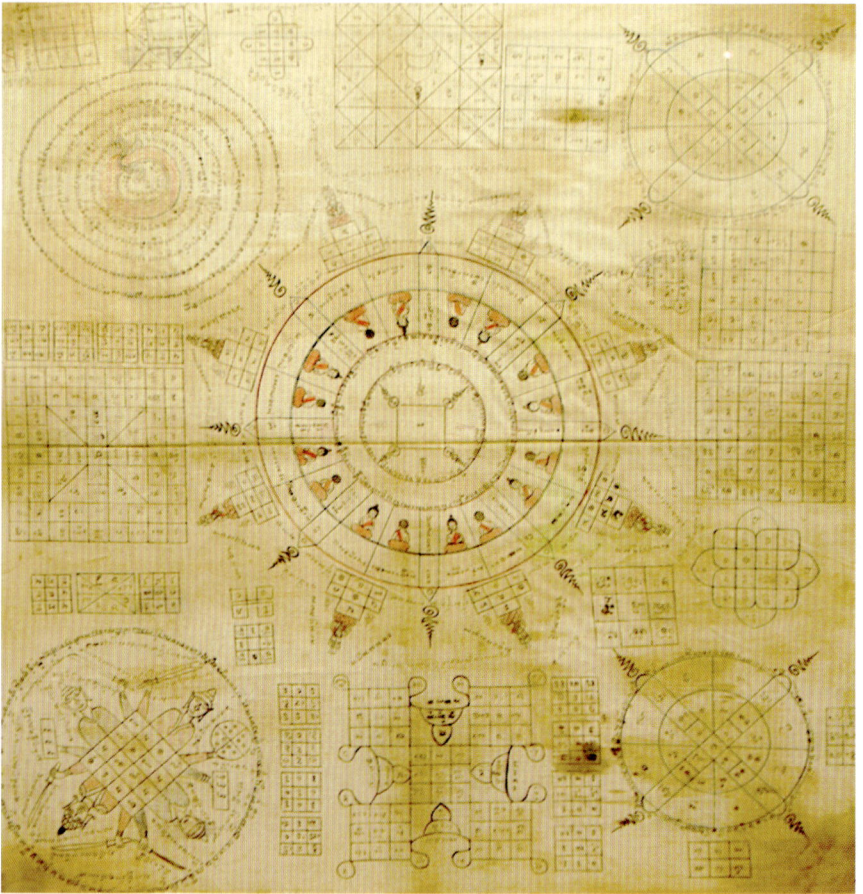

Two painted and printed mandalas on cotton cloth. Placed around them are symbols of cosmic and protective force. Collection of De Siam Antiques.

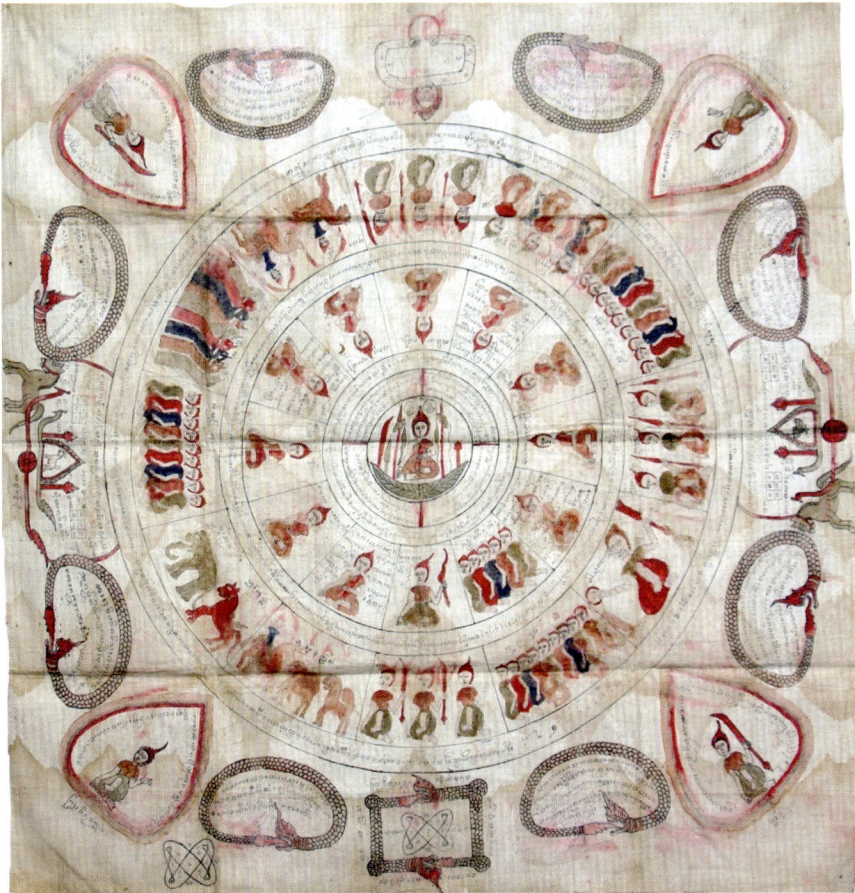

An early nineteenth century painted and printed mandala. The Buddha image is in Phra Singh Luang style.

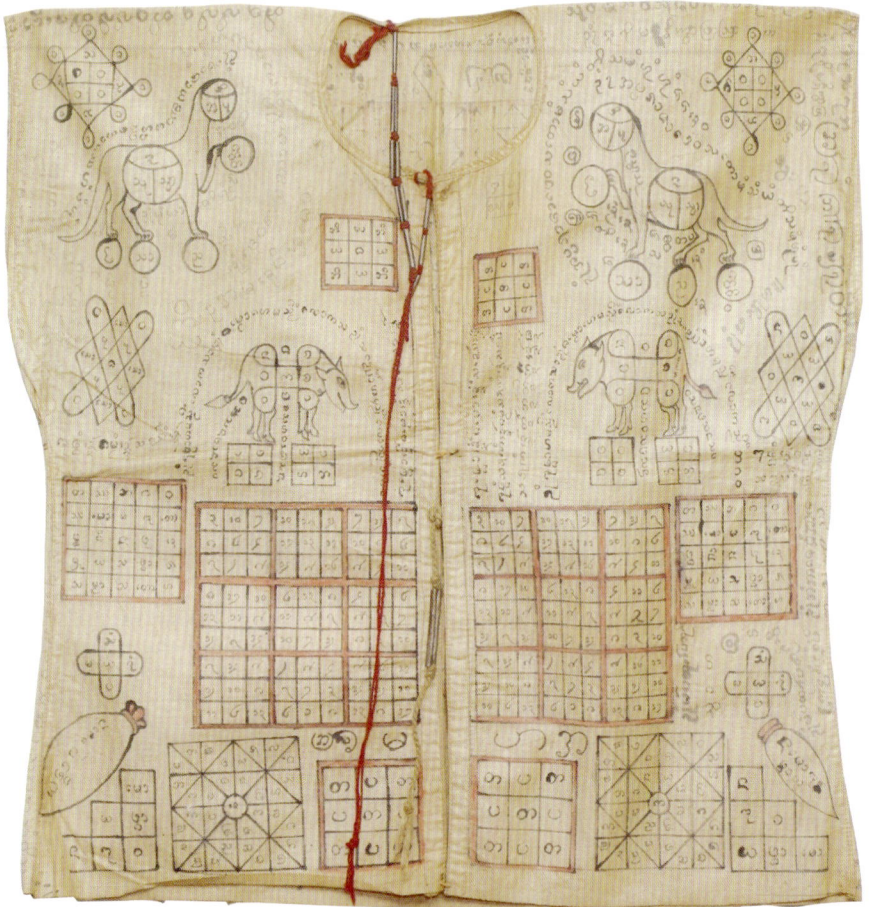

The front of a cotton talismanic shirt. The animals on the front provide protection against physical injury.

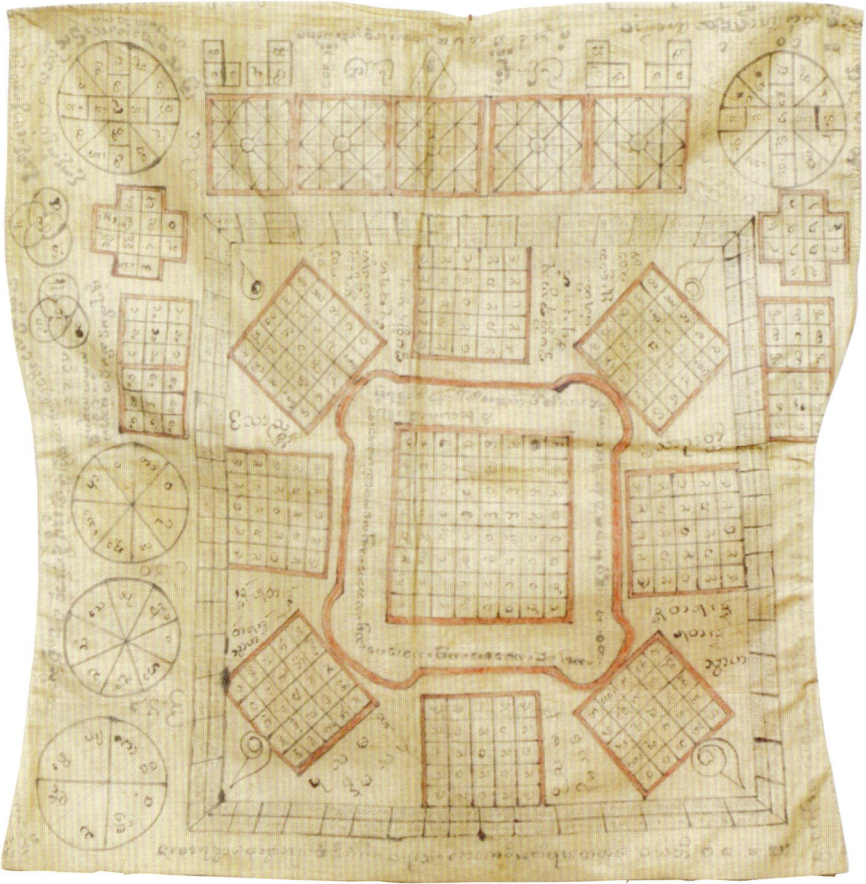

The back of the shirt with diagrams in an eight time-period formation.

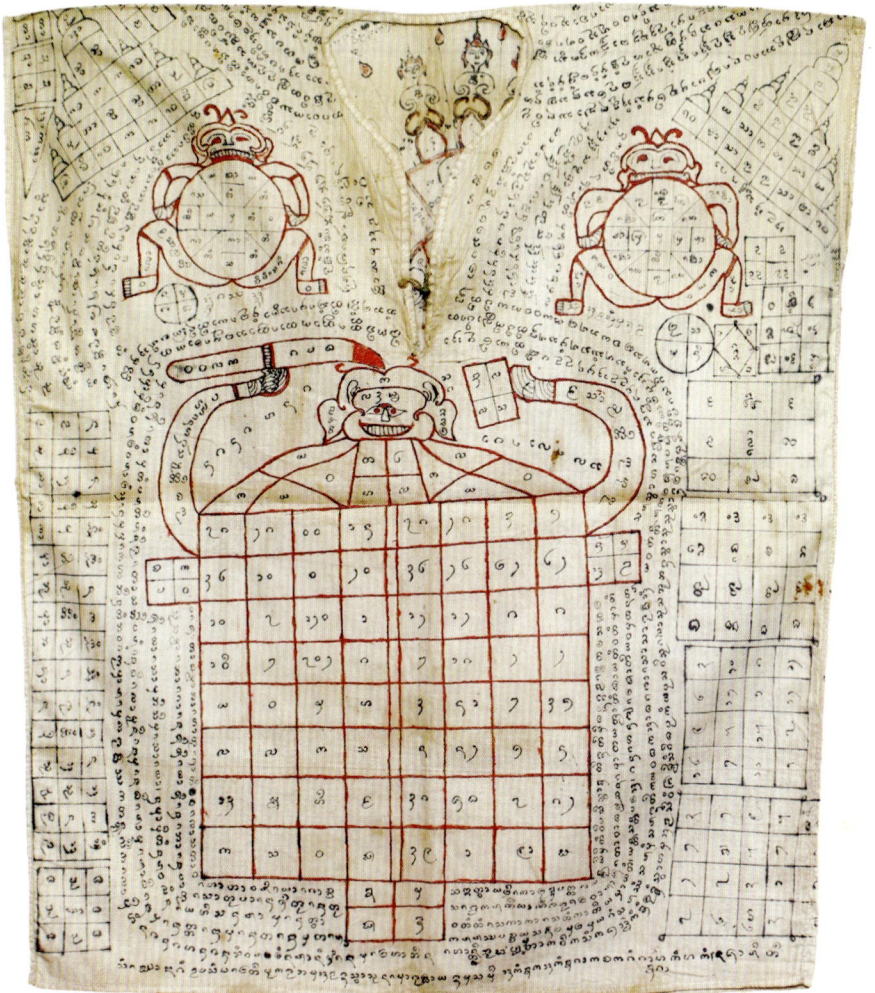

The front of a talismanic shirt. On the front the god Rahu is portrayed as a frog swallowing the moon.

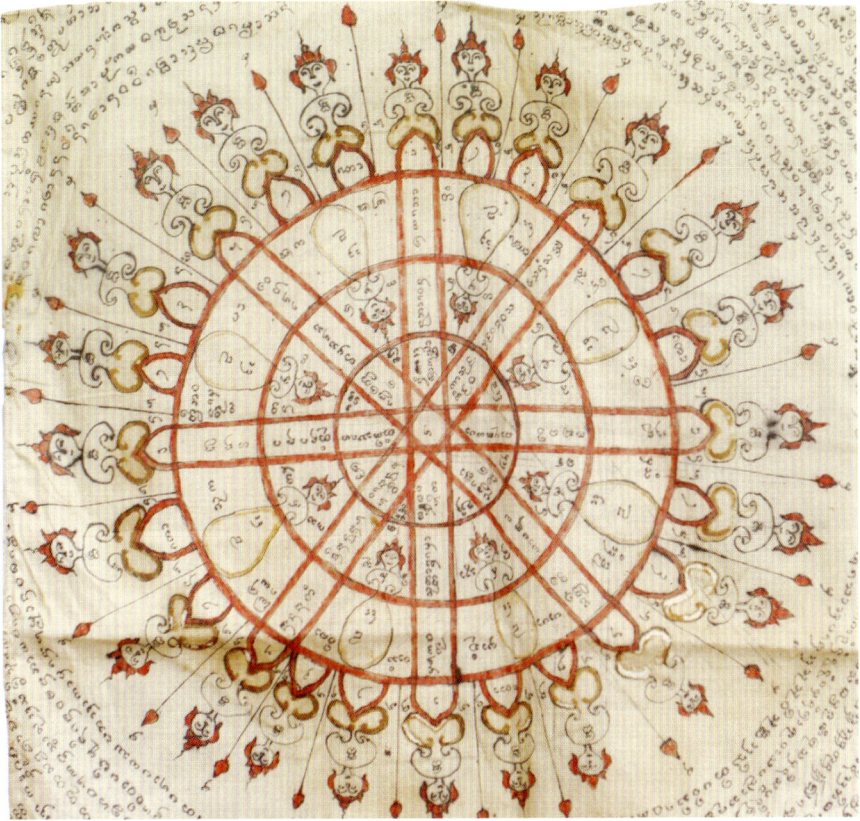

The back of a talismanic shirt. On the back is a mandala with spirits protecting the cardinal and subcardinal directions.

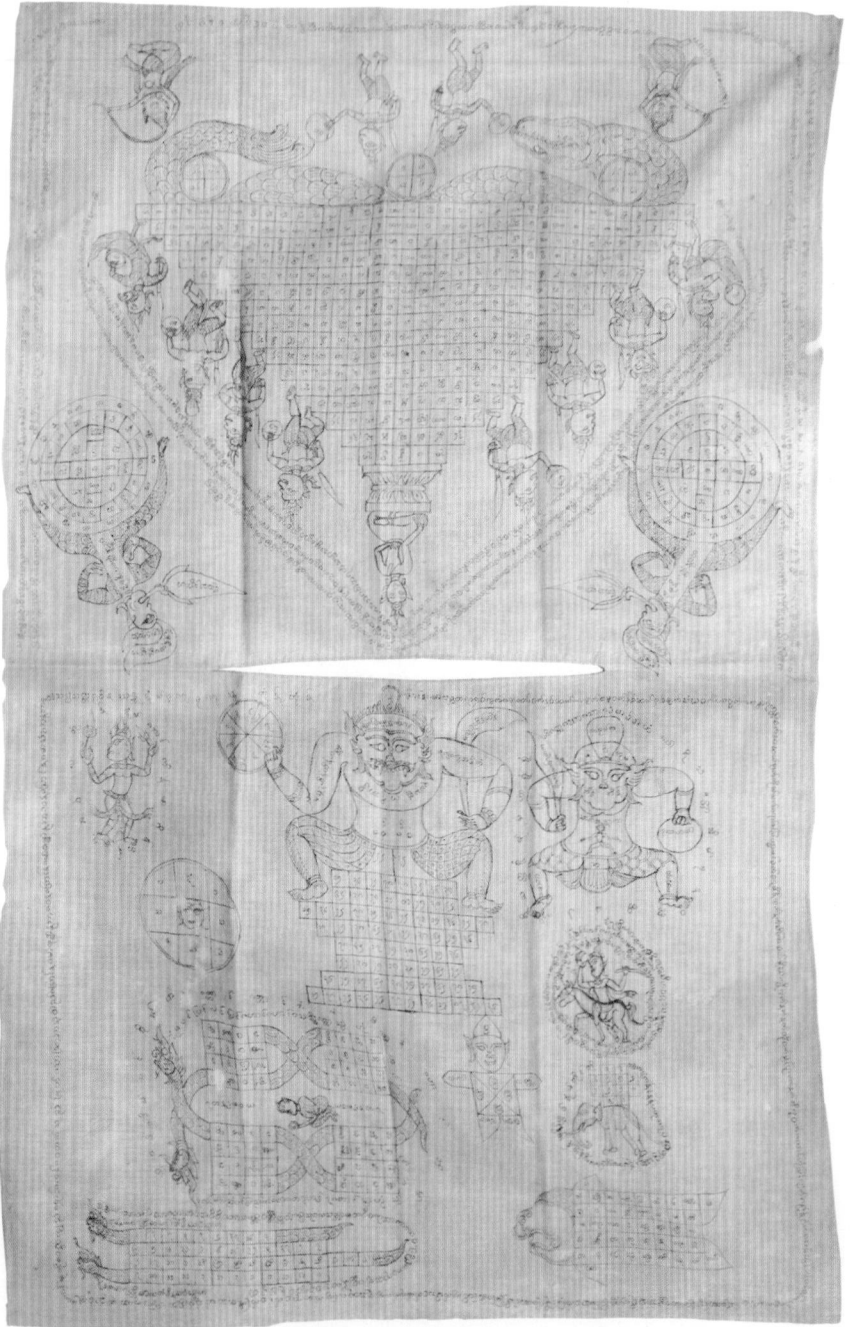

A printed cotton tabard with a slit cut as a neck opening. The iconography includes the Buddha, the god Rahu, a naga and protective spirits.

A mulberry paper love talisman featuring Phya Khaokha and his consorts. The discoloured creases indicate the paper was folded repeatedly to a size that could be concealed in the folds of a turban.

Painted and printed cotton divination chart. The diagram is based on the eight-period time system with a *naga* opposite a *garuda*, a tiger opposite a cow, a cat opposite a mouse, and a *singha* opposite an elephant, Lan Na, nineteenth century. (De Siam Antiques)

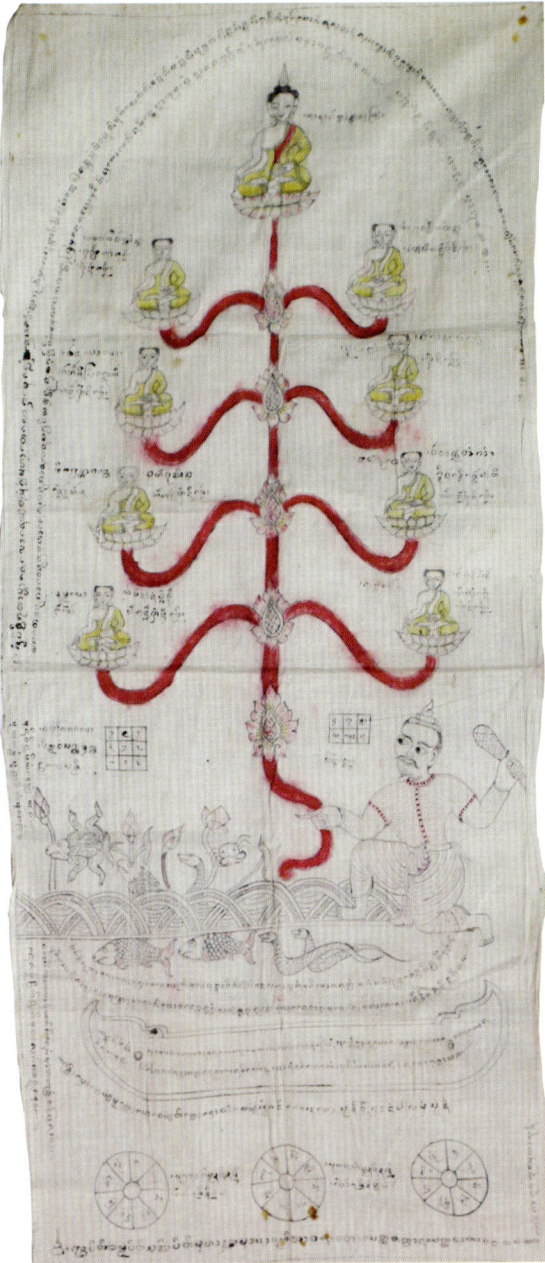

Rectangular cotton talismans for protection, *metta* and good luck. The depiction of mount Meru and its ocean-submerged base show interesting stylistic variations, nineteenth century. (De Siam Antiques)

A modern *yantra* recently prepared by a *saya* on mulberry paper using a ballpoint pen, Chiang Mai.

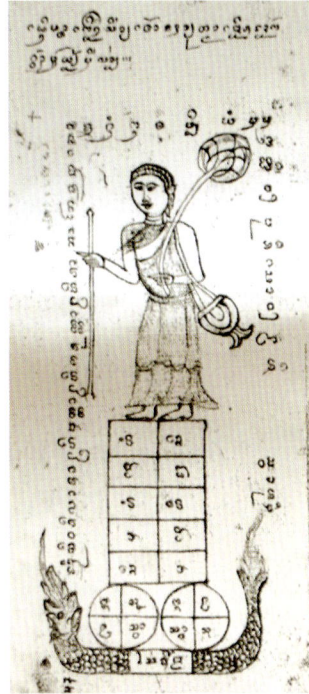

Phra Siwali represented in three manuscripts. As a beneficial cult figure he radiates metta (loving-kindness) and brings good luck. Wat Pa Daed and Wat Pa Bong, Chiang Mai and Wat Tun Tai Phayao. Microfiche Library, Archives of the Social Research Institute, Chiang Mai University.

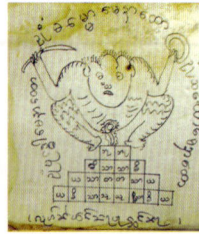

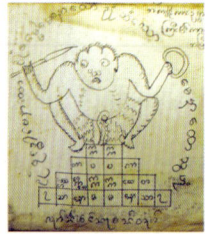

Guardian spirits of the cardinal direction. Two guardians protect the north, one protects the east and one the west. Asia Department Library of Congress, Washington DC, no. 380.

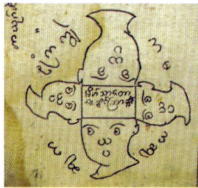

Spirits from a manuscript. Copied onto mulberry paper, which are used in healing and protection rituals.

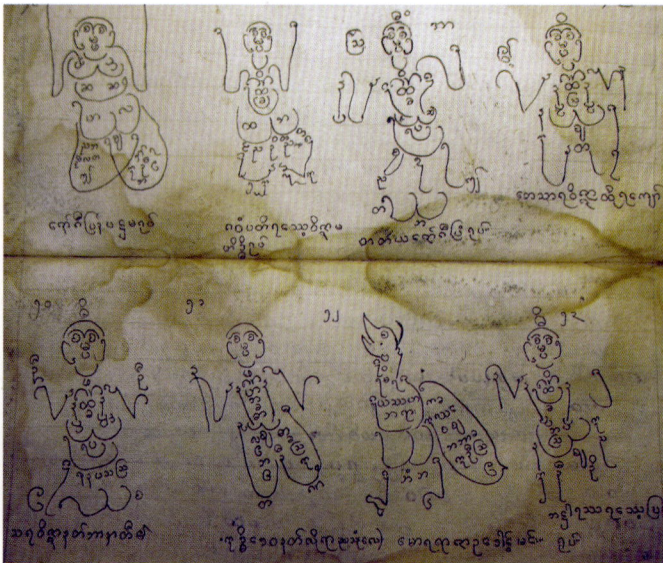

Manuscript folios with eight spirits, their bodies formed from elongated and compressed letters in Dua Tham script. They represent purity, spiritual peace, education, music and aesthetic virtue. Asia Department Library of Congress, Washington DC, no. 380.

Two symbols of good luck. Nang Kaew, represented on printed and painted cotton, brings wealth by luring customers into shops. Fork-tailed lizards in a manuscript folio are talismans for good luck.

Animal *yantra* are popular as tattoo images. The tiger brings the attributes of stealth, speed and physical force, while the pig with its thick skin brings protection from bullet wounds and injury from knives, spears and swords. Property of a *saya*, Mae Hong Son.

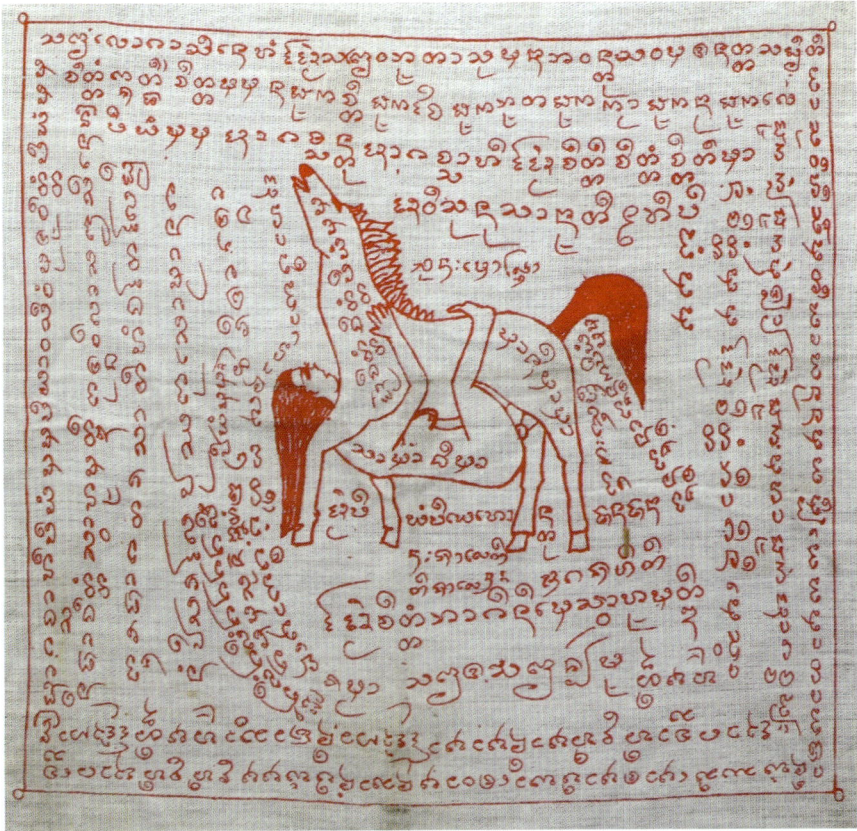

A cotton cloth portraying a woman acquiring power through the semen of a horse. A Buddhist interpretation associates the image with metta (loving-kindness).

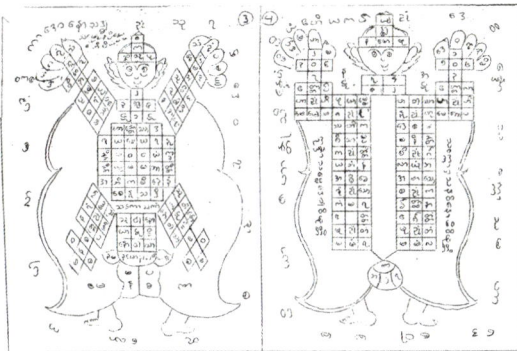

A modern *yantra* created on thin paper by a monk *saya*. He described the *yantra* as *katha* thon-pis, meaning 'to withdraw negative power'.

A folio from a manuscript on herbalism and magic, Horniman Museum and Gardens, London, catalogue no. nn 12674.

The spirit house of the senior guardian spirit (phi chao mueang) of the state of Keng Tung State.

A spirit house attached to a sacred tree growing by a river, Shan State.

An altar where offerings are made to the spirits before a tattooing session begins.

The consulting room of a *saya* in Shan State. It includes a portrait of His late Majesty King Bhumibol of Thailand.

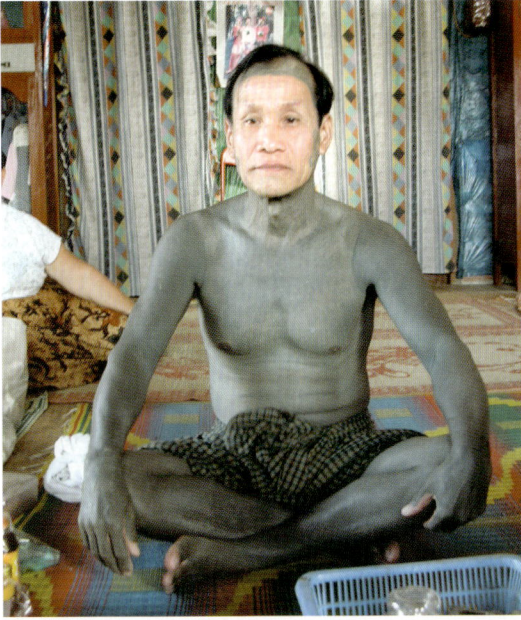

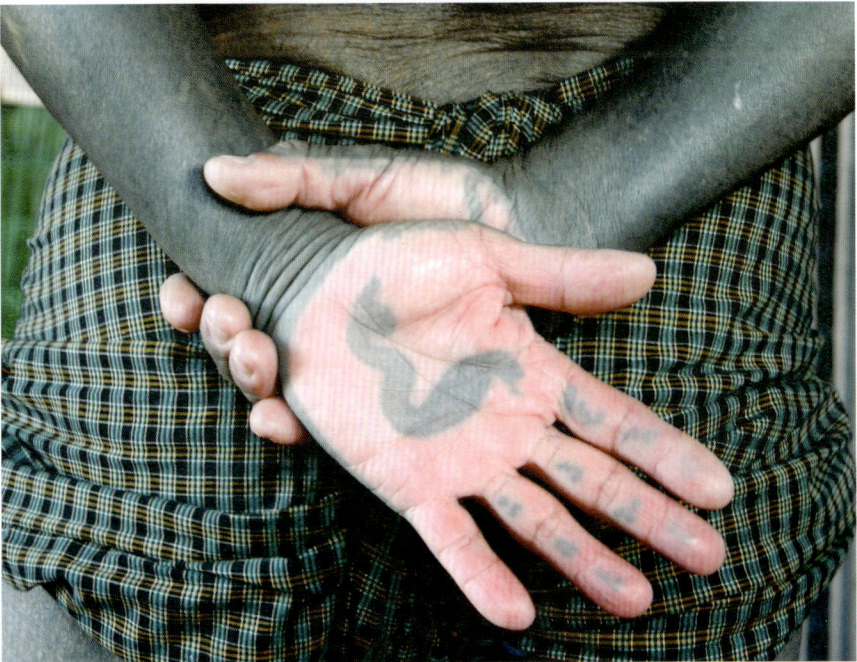

A *saya* with extensive tattoos that have turned his skin black. His face and the palms of his hands have naga tattoos.

A mural painting of men with tattoos from waist to knee, 18th–19th century, Wat Buak Khrok Luang, Chiang Mai.

A monk *saya* with a chart explaining the mathematics of cosmological force and time-period systems used in rituals for healing and protection.

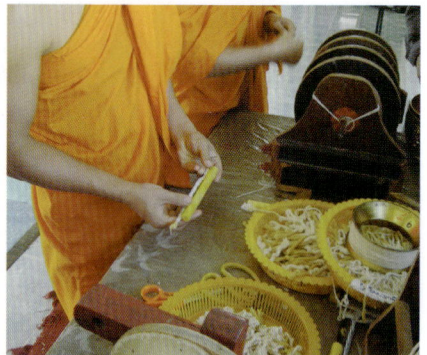

A monk preparing a ritual candle. He holds in his hands a hollow wax candle and a cotton wick bound with a *yantra* that will be inserted into the candle.

CHAPTER 2

ARTS OF THE SUPERNATURAL: ILLUSTRATIONS

In Chapter 1 spirits were described as mystical entities, capable of creating good and evil. According to Tai mythology, it was these mystical entities that revealed to *saya* a world beyond human experience. They taught *saya* how to operate in the supernatural world, transmitting the knowledge to them while they were in a state of trance.[1] This tradition continues, and spirit mediums go into trance to communicate with the spirits, their body gestures indicating when spirits respond. But there was a desire to move beyond an abstract mystical force to create tangible images, drawings and paintings that reveal what spirits look like, turning the invisible into the visible. This transition to visual images inspired a range of emotional responses, a sense of awe, fear, desire, love and repulsion. Where did Lan Na and Shan *saya* find inspiration for the strange creatures they created. Was it coming from the spirit world, inspired by dreams and hallucinations and was the living world included? This chapter explores how *saya* created tangible images and where inspiration came from.

The first spirit images were etched in roughly hewn stone and marked on cave walls. Centuries later they appear in *pap kien* (book style) and *pap tup* (leperello) manuscripts that were copied and recopied over time. Few survive from before the eighteenth century. It is possible to argue that because they were copied and recopied, nineteenth-century versions provide

---

1. Catherine Becchetti, *Le mystère dans les lettres: étude sur les yantra bouddhiques du Cambodge et de la Thaïlande*, Bangkok: Editions des cahiers de France, 1991.

an authentic historical perspective. The choice of images and how they were used was selective, either to create positive power or negative power, good or evil.

From the beginning of the Buddhist Era, positive power became associated with images of the Buddha and his followers. In terms of visual presentation, they conform to standard gestures (*mudra*) common in all forms of Buddhist art. In manuscript drawings the Buddha is presented most often in *bhumisparsha mudra*. By the fifteenth century images were based on sculptures, for example the fifteenth-century Phra Singh Luang image from Chiang Saen that significantly, in the context of this book, has supernatural healing power.[2] Images of spirits were of a complex nature. Some grotesques represent forms of negative power, but they could be turned into positive power. There is little standardisation and evil spirits, ghosts and witches are presented in many different forms.

Techniques and materials contribute to the way manuscript drawings are produced. Handmade paper is produced from mulberry bark. It has an uneven surface that affects the regularity of a line drawing. The artist works with black ink, a mix of soot and animal bile, or red made from cinnabar extracted from the rattan palm (*Daemonorops*). Other colours come from indigo and tree and plant extracts.[3] The use of a bamboo or metal stylus gives outline drawings a firm if uneven mark while fine animal-hair brushes add flourish. In present times some *saya* use notebooks for reference and make drawings in red and blue ballpoint pens; some resort to using photocopies (see Chapter 5).

When creating supernatural formulae (*yantra*), monk *saya* consult esoteric manuscripts held in monastery libraries. Lay *saya* generally have their own versions. They select images and texts for prescriptions. If a

2. This image is in Wat Phra Singh, Chiang Mai.

3. In a Buddhist context, red symbolises wisdom, virtue, good fortune and dignity. See Daniel Perdue, *The Course in Buddhist Reasoning and Debate: An Asian Approach to Analytical Thinking Drawn from Indian and Tibetan Sources*, Boston: Shambhala Publications, 2002.

particular *yantra* is not effective, it will be altered completely or have minor adjustments made to it. Some *saya* experiment continually to meet the needs of individual clients. There is evidence of this in the manuscripts where notes are scribbled by the side of *yantra*. They remind a *saya* of how a particular *yantra* was prescribed and how the client responded. Or the note reminds him of how a prescription was altered to make it more effective. If a *yantra* is used for communication with evil spirits, it is a hazardous procedure. A *saya* adds a note exonerating himself from blame if it goes wrong. This disclaimer, "I am not responsible for the evil caused by this *yantra*. I was forced against my will to use it by an army of spirit sages," is an example.

When looking for tangible sources for the physical portrayal of spirits, one starting point is mythological characters in temple mural paintings and sculptures. Common spirits wear turbans and simple loincloths whereas royal personages are clothed in coats, patterned textiles and regalia. The library of Wat Pa Daed, Chiang Mai, has a late eighteenth-century manuscript that provides an example of this style. Spirit kings and queens wear Lan Na and Shan court dress and regalia. Mythical animals are similarly attired.[4] This *yantra* is associated with victory, not in the context of warfare but spiritual strength to triumph over evil. The *saya* copies the images on mulberry paper, adds a short text, binds the paper to a candle wick and inserts it in a hollow wax candle, which is lit while Pali incantations for victory are offered.

Other visible sources include characters from Hindu and Buddhist mythology. Vishnu, the god who protects the universe, is portrayed on his mount, a Garuda, a protective force. Vishnu descends from the realm of the gods to restore cosmic order and hence his power is invoked in rituals to bring order in society. Vishnu and Garuda appear with other gods, including the ubiquitous Rahu who controls the lunar cycle. The goddess Nang Sulat Siwalee, a transformation of the Hindu goddess Salasvati, is

4. Information provided by the librarian, Wat Pa Daed, Chiang Mai, 2007.

invoked as guardian of Buddhist scriptures and patron of education and the arts. She is a popular figure among *saya* who call on her power to memorise incantations and magic spells.[5] They appeal to her on behalf of actors, public speakers and musicians at auspicious times, the most beneficial being Wednesdays and Fridays in November and Saturdays and Buddhist holy days in March.[6] *Yantra* invoking the power of Nang Sulat Siwalee are copied on mulberry paper, rolled up with a cotton wick, immersed in a shallow dish of vegetable oil and set alight. The residual ash is mixed with fresh coconut milk, sap from a fig tree, honey gathered from wild bees and sugar cane juice and administered as a drink. An alternative method is to immerse the mulberry paper in the prepared drink and leave it for a prescribed time to allow the power of the formula to be absorbed into the liquid.[7]

According to legend, the god Rahu angered Vishnu who threw a discus that severed his body completely, and that is the way he is depicted with a head, arms and no body. In a sequence of drawings that imitate the waxing and waning of the moon, Rahu slowly swallows the moon and then slowly spits it out to create one lunar cycle. In other versions, Rahu holds the moon, represented by letters, in his hands that diminish in size and then grow again. Rahu is responsible for partial eclipses, shown licking and pawing at the sun's surface.[8] When given a human face, Rahu has a moustache and eyes, nose, mouth, cheeks and ears formed from magic numbers. When farmers appeal to Rahu as a rain-maker, he is given the face of a *naga* (*poom nak kaa*) and the body of a frog, harbinger of monsoon rain. Or he appears in the usual form of head and arms and no body, with a *naga*, symbolising

5. Information provided by Lung Ae Piya Wong and Khun Tun Yee, Mae Hong Son, 2008.

6. Information provided by Khun Baan Langkhu, apprenticed to Lung Ae Piya Wong, Mae Hong Son, 2009.

7. A *saya* familiar with this ritual said that it is not as effective as when the paper is burnt and the ash mixed into the drink.

8. Shway Yoe identifies this with a Burmese version of the myth. See *The Burman: His Life and Notions*, 1882; reprint New York: W. W Norton, 1963, p. 550.

water and fertility, in proximity. When there is fear of drought, a ritual is held, and an image of Rahu appears as a frog with the moon in his mouth.[9] Another of Rahu's attributes is to give power to herbs collected at full moon when they are most effective for medicines and potions. As a god associated with healing, an image of Rahu is copied on mulberry paper and inserted with a cotton wick inside a hollow wax candle. After the candle burns, the ash is collected and mixed with water and taken by the sick as a healing drink.

Some manuscripts produced in Shan State portray spirits in Burmese court dress. Phaya Khaokha, who is a mythical prince of love, inhabits a world of romance. Seated on a royal dais shaded by fringed parasols, he embraces his wives. Graceful female courtiers are in attendance, elegant creatures wearing Burmese dress, their hair decorated with flowers. Filmy shawls cover their shoulders. Lovebirds hover above. Parrots speak with human voices and a sacred goose represents harmony. The image is copied on mulberry paper or cotton cloth and carried as a talisman concealed in the folds of a turban or loincloth or in a purse. A man who meets a woman he finds attractive strokes the surface of the talisman and utters a spell to have his feelings magically reciprocated. There is another version of Phaya Khaokha. In this form he is transformed with the head of a bull, attended by wives and courtiers. His attributes are strength and fertility, transferrable to men who copy the image on paper or cloth and carry it as a talisman.

Illustrations in Tai manuscripts show how an individual spirit is represented in several different forms from the ornate to pared-down minimalist versions. The three examples illustrated in this chapter represent the legendary magico-religious monk traveller (*dhutanga*) Phra Siwali, who personifies *metta*, loving-kindness, goodwill, benevolence and respect. Phra Siwali shares his good fortune with humans through auspicious dreams,

9. Saimong Mangrai (Sao) trans., *The Paedaeng Chronicle and the Jengtung State Chronicle*, Michigan Papers on South and Southeast Asia 19, Ann Arbor: University of Michigan Center for South and Southeast Asian Studies, 1981, pp. 194–95.

considered symbols of good luck, and wards off their nightmares, augurs of bad luck. Phra Siwali is lucky in business and a successful fundraiser for religious causes.[10] As a beneficial cult figure, Buddhists appeal to him for a share in his good fortune. Phra Siwali is recognisable in illustrations by a begging bowl, a fan and a walking cane, often augmented with a string of Buddhist prayer beads.

The three versions for comparison are taken from manuscripts in the libraries of Wat Pa Daed and Wat Pa Bong, Chiang Mai and Wat Tun Tai, Phayao.[11] The inclusion of diagrams and texts with each image indicates a prescriptive use. The Wat Pa Daed manuscript presents Phra Siwali with an expression of gentleness and a calm bearing, his robes hanging in neat, ordered folds. The artist has drawn Phra Siwali according to the description given in the Pali text written next to him. It is from the *Metta Sutta* found in the Pali Canon and defines qualities of sincerity, gentleness, humility and honesty that are fundamental to achieving *metta*. Phra Siwali is also given high status as he stands inside a tiered palace building (*prasad*), symbol of mount Meru. The *prasad* is filled with a grid of seventy-two squares containing letters and syllables in Tham Lan Na script. The phrase *om*, an abbreviation of the sacred mantra *om mani padme hum*, is contained in a set of small stupas.[12] A *prasad* on the opposite folio is formed from one hundred and eight squares to represent the one hundred and eight auspicious symbols of the Buddha's footprint.

The second illustration is from a manuscript in the library of Wat Pa Bong. In this illustration there is a sense of movement, signifying his role as a magico-religious traveller. He is a sprightly young monk with a smiling face. A lightness of touch is echoed in his flowing summer robes. He holds

10. According to legend, Phra Siwali was carried in his mother's womb for seven years and she gave birth after seven days of labour.

11. Microfiche records, Department of Social Science, Chiang Mai University.

12. The sound *om* is described as a root of language that echoes and reverberates in perpetuity across the cosmos.

a lotus-shaped fan while jauntily swinging a begging bowl and holding a walking cane in his right hand. The background is unlike the previous example; there is no *prasad* as Phra Siwali stands on a simple rectangular dais divided into ten squares containing Tham Lan Na letters. Astrological references are presented in circles representing the planets and phases of the moon. A *naga*, symbolising water and fertility, indicates that Phra Siwali bestows good fortune for a successful harvest.

The third illustration is from a manuscript in Wat Tun Tai. It takes a minimalist approach. The body of Phra Siwali is reduced to a rectangle in a stiff, shapeless robe. His face and features are a caricature. Phra Siwali carries a begging bowl, a set of Buddhist prayer beads and a pronged fork. The latter is a symbol generally associated with the mythical monk, Phra Malai, also a traveller who visits the Buddhist heavens and hells and returns to earth to warn against the horrors of hell. This image appears to be a fusion of Phra Siwali and Phra Malai. There are other examples of spirits combined in one image, perhaps to bring the greatest benefit to those who invoke their power.

The power of Phra Siwali is invoked during candle rituals held for individual worshippers or for groups. An image is copied on mulberry paper with an accompanying text. The name of the devotee, or the names of the group, and the day, year and times of birth are added. This is required so the spirits can identify those taking part. The mulberry paper is folded and rolled around a cotton wick, bound with cotton cord and inserted inside a hollow wax candle. The number of folds in the paper, the ply of the candlewick and the number of bindings are calculated according to the birth data provided. An auspicious time to light the candle is synchronised with the lunar cycle. Verses of a Pali text dedicated to the Buddha and Phra Siwali are chanted while the candle burns.[13] Incantations include "I revere

---

13. Stanley Jeyaraja Tambiah, *The Buddhist Saints of the Forest and the Cult of Amulets*, Cambridge: Cambridge University Press, 1984, pp. 24–25.

the Buddha-jewel highest balm and best, ever beneficial to gods and men. By that Buddha's glory may all obstacles and suffering cease".[14]

If the ritual is organised by a group, each member holds a hollow wax candle filled with a wick, the portrait of Siwali and their name and birth data. The candle is bound with lotus flowers. The group chants the Pali text. In some cases, a group orders one large candle to share. The cost of beeswax, which is expensive, is divided among the participants, and they also donate to the monastery. Offerings are made to the spirits and the cost of these offerings of uncooked rice, white cloth, red cloth, fruit, flowers, cigarettes and joss sticks is shared. Devotees gather round the candle to chant in Pali and in local dialect while it burns.

Some spirits are ugly creatures, deformed monsters with human and animal parts. Like Rahu, some do not have a body, often only a distorted head with twisted features, one ear and jagged teeth, or a grotesque face with eyes and nose formed from letters and blurred lines of script as a disfigured jawline. Villagers describe encounters with such spirit monsters when alone in the forest or walking in the dark away from home. Although they can be seen as portents of evil, such images are also prescribed to frighten other evil spirits, particularly those causing illness. A monster image is copied on mulberry paper and inserted in a beeswax candle. The residual ash is collected and dissolved in water and administered to a patient as a drink. Alternately, the mulberry paper is soaked in water for a specified time that allows the power of the image to flow into the water. The patient drinks the water.[15]

Some healing rituals require a sacred space created around a patient, delineated with a cordon of white cotton thread. To prevent evil spirits entering the space, protection is provided by the spirits of the cardinal

---

14. In Pali *sakkatvā Buddha ratanam, osadham uttamam varam, Hitam deva manussanam-Buddha tejena sotthina Nassantu paddava sabbe dukkha vupasamentu me.*

15. Information provided by a *saya*, Mae Hong Son, January 2010.

and four subcardinal directions. Numbers four or eight are chosen for the number of *yantra*, and ritual materials are prepared, for example a *yantra* of four spirit heads on four sides of a square representing north, south, east and west. The facial features are formed from letters representing protective incantations. The drawing is copied on four sheets of mulberry paper immersed in four bowls of sesame oil. Four wicks made from eight-ply cotton are inserted in the bowls of oil. Each is placed on an eight-legged stand, positioned in the cardinal directions, and the wicks are lit while protective incantations are offered.

Tai rulers were responsible for protection of land and people against enemy invasion, disease epidemics and natural disasters such as floods and drought, thought of as punishment by evil spirits. Rulers employed *saya* to conduct rituals for protection within established land boundaries and around cities. The Chiang Mai and Nan chronicles record the founding of the Lan Na kingdom in the thirteenth century, with cities built with brick walls and moats as protection against enemy forces. Rituals were held at the time foundation stones were laid. The chronicles state that three foundation stones were laid, one for the spirits dwelling at the site, the second for animal spirits nearby and the third for guardian spirits that protect the city gates. There is no record of the materials used, but a foundation stone recovered at the site of the thirteenth-century city of Chiang Rai is in cruciform shape, made of brick and incised with an image of a guardian spirit.

Protective *yantra* were incised in wood, brick and metal and set in boundary walls and above city gates. Protective icons made of wood were set in niches in city walls. The woods selected as auspicious were *mai teng* (*Shorea obtusa*) and *mai rang* (*Pentacme siamensis*). *Yantra* and icons were produced in sets for each of the cardinal directions.[16] Accompanying texts

16. Wood relates to the Year of the Tiger and the Year of the Rabbit. It is scented, dry, hard mountain wood.

give instructions on their exact placement.[17] Protective *yantra* were drawn and painted in gold leaf at the entrance to important buildings within the city. An example of a *yantra* of this type is a square diagram containing astrological symbols, Pali texts written in shorthand and lucky numbers in Tai script. Pali incantations and magic spells were chanted at the time of installation.

A manuscript from the Library of Congress, Washington DC, contains a set of guardian spirits portrayed as anthropomorphic creatures with distorted features. They are similar in form but not identical. Two spirits protect the north and one each the west and east. There is no guardian of the south. The guardian of the east has the body of a frog holding a slingshot in the right hind leg and a thunderbolt in the left. The north and west guardians hold daggers in their right hands and thunderbolts in their left. Facial features are formed from letters. Protuberances shaped like umbilical cords connect each spirit to a gridded dais containing Pali words and phrases. A set of letters are shorthand for "May the Buddha be my refuge, May the dhamma be my refuge, May the sangha be my refuge". Instructions are given for two images to be buried in a northerly direction, one towards the west and one towards the east. These instructions are similar to those given for other protective spirits, such as three stones, not four, laid as foundation stones, three directions, not four, for *yantra* on paper. The three foundation stones laid were, as in the previous instructions taken from the chronicles, one for the spirits dwelling at the site, the second for animal spirits nearby and the third for guardian spirits that protect city gates.

Although there is a history of three foundation stones for Tai cities, there are four guardian spirits of the cardinal directions, and they were often named during protective rituals. In Chiang Mai, the Lan Na guardian spirits are Surajato, who protects the West, Gandharakkhito the North, Sulakkhito

17. Information provided by the monks of Wat Jong Kham, Keng Tung, 2011.

the East and Jayabhumo the South.[18] In Keng Tung, Shan State, the guardians are Tatharattha, who protects the East, Virurakkha the South, Virupakka the West and Kuvera the North.[19]

One of the most popular spirits in Shan State is *phi lo*, who expels evil spirits that possess humans. *Phi lo* is a frightening creature wearing a halo of flames. He has red eyes, prominent teeth and curled fangs protruding from exaggerated hairy lips. He has no neck, an indication of a lower being. His chest is broad and tapers to a belted waist above a short loincloth. He brandishes knives that resemble meat cleavers, symbols of cannibalism.[20] The word *yakka* identifies him as a spirit. Illustrations of *phi lo* are produced as a *yantra* with a Pali text enclosing the image. The text is an important component because *phi lo* is an unpredictable spirit with power that can spiral out of control. A Pali text is a means of restraint. *Phi lo* is a spirit of last resort for patients who sought treatment elsewhere without success. His image is copied on mulberry paper with the name of the patient and the day, time and year of birth. A fragment of clothing is included with the paper and candle wick, bound together with cotton cord.[21] This elongated bundle is rolled in softened beeswax to form a candle and lit at a time specified by the *saya*, calculated according to the patient's birth data.[22] Protective incantations (*ang hae kwang*) and good luck incantations (*thien suk lap luk wan*) are offered while the candle burns.

18. Sommai Premchit and Amphay Doré, *The Lan Na Twelve-month Traditions: An Ethno-historic and Comparative Approach*, Research Report, Faculty of Social Sciences, Chiang Mai University, Thailand, and Centre National de la Recherche Scientifique, France, 1991, pp. 230–32.

19. Information provided by Phra Yee Noon, Wat Suan Dork, Chiang Mai, February 2012.

20. Kraisri Nimmaenhaeminda has written on the cannibalistic nature of spirits in Chiang Mai. See 'The Lawa Guardian Spirits of Chiangmai', *Journal of the Siam Society* 55(2): 185–225.

21. A photograph of the person may be substituted for a fragment of clothing.

22. One of the eight time periods (see Chapter 1).

A similar ritual that places emphasis on protection involves copying four images of *phi lo* on four separate sheets of mulberry paper, which are then rolled and bound to cotton wicks and immersed in four bowls of sesame oil. They are placed in the cardinal directions. The patient lies with the head facing east and the feet to the west, and Pali incantations are chanted as the wicks burn. Residual ash is collected and mixed with water which the patient drinks. *Phi lo* has the power to help those seeking to overcome negative spirits creating obstacles to success, for example students sitting examinations. In Keng Tung market small blocks of *sompoy*, a type of soap distilled from *Acacia rugata Mer.*, are stamped with images of *phi lo*. You buy a cake of soap, wash your face with it in a cleansing ritual and negative spirits are dispelled.

Particularly realistic drawings of spirits can project mood, either in the stance of the figure or the facial expression. Emotion shown in a face is achieved in the placement of contorted letters, for example a sense of fear and anxiety projected in a *yantra* of seven faces in a circular illustration with an accompanying text. The *yantra* is for treating anxious patients who have already consulted a doctor but not received a diagnosis. A *saya* copies the *yantra* on four separate sheets of mulberry paper, folded according to directions given in an accompanying text. To ensure that spirits recognise the patient, a fragment of their clothing or a photograph is included with the mulberry paper. The sheets are immersed in four shallow bowls of sesame oil and placed in the cardinal directions at the head, feet and on each side of the patient whose head faces east and feet west. The papers are lit and incantations offered over a period of four days, the exact time calculated according to the patient's birth data. In this treatment, the residue ash is impure and disposed of far from the patient, usually on derelict land.

Saya know that one treatment with a *yantra* may not produce a result. It may be necessary to perform several rituals. After the first attempt, a stronger *yantra* is selected. This involves distorted human figures ringed with spells and magic symbols. Images are copied on mulberry paper, rolled and bound to a wick not made from cotton but from plied threads drawn from a worn male sarong, and immersed in a shallow bowl of vegetable oil. The accompanying instructions stipulate two centilitres of oil. Chanting takes place while the wick burns. The *saya* waits for a time to see if the patient has responded. If there is no sign of improvement, the *saya* knows he is dealing with a particularly powerful spirit and performs a third ritual. The four contorted figures are copied on sheets of mulberry paper, the number of sheets calculated according to the patient's birth data. The sheets are immersed in bowls of oil, prepared as in the second prescription and placed around the patient's bed. Pali incantations and magic spells are chanted while the paper burns. The residual ash is collected and eaten mixed with easily digested vegetarian food. If there is still no sign of recovery, the *saya* resorts to calling on a spirit medium for an exorcism at a nearby spirit house or in the grounds of a cemetery. The treatment involves the medium luring away evil spirits reluctant to leave the patient. Tempting offerings laid on a bamboo tray include flowers, betel ingredients, green tea, uncooked rice and two-kyat coins. The tray is positioned far away from the patient and the medium calls the spirits to come and accept the offerings prepared on the tray.

If the spirits still refuse to leave the patient, the *saya* performs another ritual that involves the active participation of the patient. An image of a particularly ugly ogre with crossed eyes, prominent nose, grimacing mouth and rows of irregular teeth is copied on mulberry paper with a magic spell written on the cheekbones. It is folded, rolled with a cotton wick, immersed in a bowl of oil and carried to a cemetery where the patient is waiting. The wick is lit and the patient calls to the sprits "Venerable sirs, I am here". If they fail to respond, the patient is taken home, too ill to be moved again. As a last resort, the *saya* calls the spirits to the patient's bedside. He uses the drawing of the ogre and rings a Shan metal bell with a distinctive resounding echo believed to attract spirits. The ogre is copied on mulberry paper and immersed in a bowl of oil and placed under the bed. The patient chants "Venerable sirs, I am here".

Animal Spirits

Before the destruction of local forests, the people of Lan Na and Shan State were confronted with dangerous wild animals and were familiar with their characteristics and habits, which they treated with great respect. Those entering the forests to hunt and traders travelling through were careful to protect themselves against attack. They lit fires, climbed trees and carried protective talismans. But it was not just the ferocious nature of wild animals that commanded respect. They recognised other valuable characteristics, such as the agility, dexterity and intelligence of monkeys, the stealth of snakes, the cunning and stealth of civet cats and the impenetrable skin of wild pigs. These were attributes they wanted magically transferred to them. They consulted *saya* who knew the necessary *yantra* and incantations to make it happen.

Most in demand among hunters were the characteristics of a tiger, its fearlessness, stealth, strength and speed in attack. To acquire those attributes, *saya* created a range of tiger talismans based on images copied from manuscripts. The power of the tiger is accentuated in its pouncing stance, back legs extended, jaws open, sharp teeth ready to attack. Or the tiger stands, jaws open, teeth visible, body stiff, surrounded by an array of powerful symbols and magic spells. A *saya* selects a suitable image and an accompanying text of incantations and spells and copies them on mulberry paper or cotton cloth or they are carved in wood or semiprecious stones concealed as a talisman in a turban or pocket. When confronted by a tiger, the image is stroked and a spell chanted to magically gain courage to confront the tiger and force it to retreat. Tiger tattoos and tiger shirts carry similar power (see Chapters 5 and 6). Tiger talismans were treated carefully and could be put to bad use, particularly by young men to create aggression, violence and recklessness.[23]

To have the power and stealth of a tiger is a powerful attribute, but other animal characteristics were valued. A civet cat was recognised for its cunning and stealth, and a *yantra* of a civet cat was popular with soldiers in battle and escaped criminals trying to evade recapture. It was a popular tattoo image (see Chapter 6). A *yantra* acting as a talisman portrays a civet cat with a Pali incantation, *namo buddhaya* (hail to the Buddha). Wild pigs were respected for their fearless natures and thick, impenetrable skins, credited with resisting bullet wounds, cuts from knives, spears and swords, and the bites and tearing claws of wild animals. *Yantra* of wild pigs are figurative drawings with incantations and magic spells inside and around their bodies. In some *yantra* the animal is barely discernible among diagrams, canopies and lotus blossoms, a version reputed to be the most effective in protection against enemy attack.[24] A ritual using a wild pig *yantra* copied on mulberry paper involves setting it alight in a bowl of vegetable oil. The residual ash is dissolved in water and given as a drink or blended with oil and herbs and rubbed into the skin. Instructions say that a time lag of a week is needed before it is fully functioning and the skin impenetrable.

It is not only wild animals that have characteristics magically adopted by humans; it also applies to farm animals. The water buffalo, a common sight in the rice fields of Southeast Asia, is a resilient animal used for pulling heavy ploughs and laden farm carts. By nature, it is unpredictable and has a reputation for frightening the spirits. It was a popular *yantra* for soldiers going into battle. The image was copied on mulberry paper with a set of magic spells and swallowed with water. Or it was copied on mulberry paper and rolled with a cotton wick in a bowl of sesame oil, set alight, the ash collected and dissolved in water for soldiers to drink, or mixed with oil and

23. Interview with Gaysorn and Kan-na Rubnamtham, Mae Hong Son, January 2010.
24. *Ibid.*

ground herbs rubbed into the skin. A week was allowed for the treatment to take effect. In contrast to the unpredictability of water buffalo, the cow is considered dependable and vigilant. To acquire these attributes, a *yantra* is prepared with an image of a cow drawn in outline and magic letters form the head, features and legs. The hooves are drawn using the syllable *da*, meaning 'vigilance'.

A fork-tailed lizard (*i cawk*) is a popular *yantra* as it brings luck to a house and its occupants. The lizard lives in the house and is recognised by its loud, distinctive call. The forked tail is fundamental to good luck. If a lizard is found dead with its tail intact, the tail becomes a lucky talisman and is kept in the house in a jar of preserving fluid.[25] Manuscripts containing lizard *yantra* have accompanying incantations and spells. A spell written by the side of the lizard's mouth is phonic and mimics the lizard's lucky call. The *yantra* is copied on mulberry paper and carried as a talisman. It was popular among Shan traders who before the era of paved roads travelled with their laden bullocks and ponies through narrow mountain passes and malaria-infested forests, subject to attack by bandits and wild animals. When traders sensed danger, they stroked the lizard *yantra* while offering incantations for protection. This *yantra* also had power to create kindness and goodwill among strangers in the towns and villages that traders passed through.

If an owl flies into a house, it is a sign of impending bad luck as evil spirits take the opportunity to fly in with the owl. To exorcise the spirits, a *yantra* with a square diagram and a bird perched on it is drawn on a freshly picked banana leaf and placed on an offering tray with a slice of fruitcake. It is set outside the house at the exact spot where the owl flew in. A magic spell is chanted thirty-seven times to entice the spirit out.[26] As it is not known which spirit has entered, the chant is addressed to each spirit individually for all thirty-seven spirits in the Shan pantheon.

25. Information provided by Kham Indra, Chiang Mai University, 2009.
26. Becchetti, pp. 23–24.

An erotic image of a woman having sexual intercourse with a horse is interpreted by monks as a *yantra* for *metta* (loving-kindness), fidelity and devotion. It represents the legend of a husband who dies, and his *karma* leads him to be reborn as a horse. His devoted wife recognises the horse as her reincarnated husband. They continue a loving relationship, illustrated in the image as sexual intercourse. Both are encircled with a Pali incantation, *metta piyam ma ma* ("love to me"). Women and animals engaging in sexual activity appear in other *yantra* on paper and cloth, as a tattoo image and in painted effigies in wood and stone. According to local folklore, the image is not an expression of high moral value, but a sign of power transferred through semen. It can be from a horse, an elephant or a *kinnara* (a mythical half-human half-bird representing the power of celestial musicians, poets, dancers and singers) or *naga*. This belief extends to the animal kingdom with power being transferred from the strong to the weak, for example a mouse sucking semen from the penis of a tiger.

This chapter has so far focused on figurative drawings illustrated in outline with letters added as facial features, but there are *yantra* of human and animal spirits formed entirely from letters of the alphabet acting as shorthand for magic spells. Letters are elongated and shortened, enlarged or compressed to form facial features, the body, limbs and internal organs. There is a unique quality to the drawings as they are part of a specific coding system. It is argued that the drawings are produced while in a trance-like state, chanting while drawing the letters.[27] The process of creating images in this way gives scope for whimsical and bizarre figures, for example creatures formed from stacks of letters with insect heads. The resulting images are described by *saya* as magic spells for protection. They can be chanted into the open palm of the hand. The hand is then formed into a clenched fist, pointed in the direction of an adversary, then opened and directed towards

---

27. Informants stress this incantation is for protection only and cannot be used to bring harm to an adversary. Interview with monks at Wat Tiyasathan, Chiang Mai Province.

him. If an individual is too afraid to make such a direct confrontation, the words of the magic spell can be whispered into the palm of the hand which is held over the mouth.

Prescribed drawings forming the words of magic spells appear in sets dealing with specific aspects of magic. The Library of Congress, Washington DC owns a Shan manuscript containing a set of forty-eight *yantra* on twelve consecutive folios of a manuscript. In one section the *yantra* are for musicians, actors, dancers, public speakers and their instructors. An image of the Buddha represents the cleansing power of fire, bringing purity and spiritual peace to performers. Next is a *kinnari*, and two *kinnari*. They speak with soft, persuasive voices. The next folio portrays *navassakuna kinnara* who has power in the performing arts, followed by *visavija takkasila rishi*, a god appeased by educators. *Ekeavisati* is a tiger embodying physical and mental strength required for long periods of artistic performance, and the brahmin Bharivisati is a strong, determined spirit and symbol of academic achievement. Clients select the appropriate spirit whose attributes they wish to acquire. For example, a performer may ask for a copy of a *kinnari* and *kinnara* copied on mulberry paper by a *saya*, rolled with a cotton wick and lit in a bowl of oil. The residual ash is collected and mixed with fresh coconut milk, sugar cane juice and honey from wild bees as a drink. The potion gives a performer a smooth tone of voice that audiences enjoy, and it is effective for up to five hours.

Other *yantra* from this Library of Congress manuscript bring attributes associated with education. A king *garuda* is a symbol of victory and brings endurance to those studying for long periods to achieve good examination results. A *yantra* with a Buddha image imparts attentiveness and concentration in students. Another Buddha *yantra* imbues a cool, calm and detached temperament to a scholar who gains the ability to correctly assess research. A popular *yantra* for students, professors and teachers features Gavampati, a legendary scholar and devout follower of the Buddha who served as one of his advisors.

In contrast to the *yantra* created for positive effect are *yantra* produced by *maw paeng* to inflict harm. An example is an outline drawing of four kneeling female figures supporting a nine-square diagram containing coded evil spells. The *yantra* is prepared on mulberry paper with the victim's name and birth data. It is rolled up tightly with a fragment of cloth taken from the face of a corpse and set alight in a bowl of oil. Evil spells are chanted while it burns. The residual ash is collected by the *maw paeng* and taken to be scattered at a site where evil spirits dwell.

A crouched male figure with a menacing expression and foreign facial features holds a sword in each hand and squats menacingly over the corpse of a child laid in a coffin. An accompanying magic spell is written in Burmese letters. This *yantra* is created to retaliate against a liar who gives false evidence against an innocent victim in court. The unfair conviction leads to a jail sentence. This *yantra* can also be formulated against deceivers who spread false rumours that ruin the reputation of a blameless individual. The power of the *yantra* lies in causing illness or an accident to the wrongdoers. The *yantra* is copied on mulberry paper with the name and birth data of the wrongdoers and wrapped in the top leaf taken from a banana tree. It is buried in the grounds of a cemetery or inserted inside an insect nest. Raw meat is offered to evil spirits at the site. The *maw paeng* chants an evil spell while focusing his thoughts on the houses where the evildoers live. There is another prescription used for the same purpose, but in this case the *yantra* is not buried but fed to a cow while the same magic spells are chanted.

A *yantra* that can cause unspecified harm to an innocent victim involves a drawing of a man wearing a turban, with facial features formed from letters. His body is a square diagram containing letters and numbers. His arms and legs are spread apart. A spell in Shan script is written by the side of the figure. This *yantra* is copied on mulberry paper with the name and birth data of the intended victim and rolled up with a fragment of his clothing. The package is buried by a *maw paeng* at a site where evil spirits dwell. He chants evil spells during the burial. Within two weeks the named individual will become insane and eventually commit suicide.

To enable one person to totally dominate and intimidate another requires a *yantra* of an ogre with features formed from elongated and compressed Burmese letters, the teeth a row of numbers. A magic spell is written around the figure. A *maw paeng* copies the drawing on mulberry paper and adds the name and birth data of the victim. He inserts the paper in a bowl of sesame oil and carries it to a cemetery. He lights the paper and shouts the name of the victim loud enough so evil spirits will hear. This *yantra* can also be used to enable one person to totally control another person. The victim becomes a slave directed to perform evil and vindictive acts on behalf of the controller. This is considered a particularly evil *yantra*. Written by the side of it is a note from a *maw paeng* claiming he is not to blame for the evil it causes as he was coerced by eighty thousand evil sages.

Performing rituals to activate evil *yantra* involves taking them to cemeteries or other sites where evil spirits are believed to be active. This creates a certain amount of risk for the *maw paeng* as evil spirits can be aggressive and turn on him or cause havoc in his community. He will be blamed for disturbing the spirits to cause drunkenness, fighting and disorderly behaviour at religious ceremonies and the harassment of monks. Attracting evil spirits can also involve prescriptions containing polluted ingredients that may physically harm the *maw paeng*. They include rusty nails, human bodily fluids, corpse fluids, animal parts, animal excrement and insects. Manuscripts contain warning signs. One of them, described as a 'crematorium spirit', has a human body and threatens with daggers. The pupil of one eye is shaped like a skull.

Maw paeng claim that powerful aggressive prescriptions are operated within a strict code. The victim must be an evil person who deserves to suffer. Permitted targets are those who cause serious physical and mental harm to others as well as those who damage or destroy the property of others on at least three occasions. Those who live honest lives and observe at least five Buddhist precepts are not victimised. If black magic is aimed at an innocent person of high moral standing, that person will suffer no ill effects because their faith will protect them. However, this code is operated according to *karma*. Those who live blameless lives in this life cycle may be targeted if they committed serious offences in a previous life.

A sleeveless cotton shirt with a snarling tiger and nine cats whose physical and mental attributes can be magically transmitted to the wearer of the shirt.

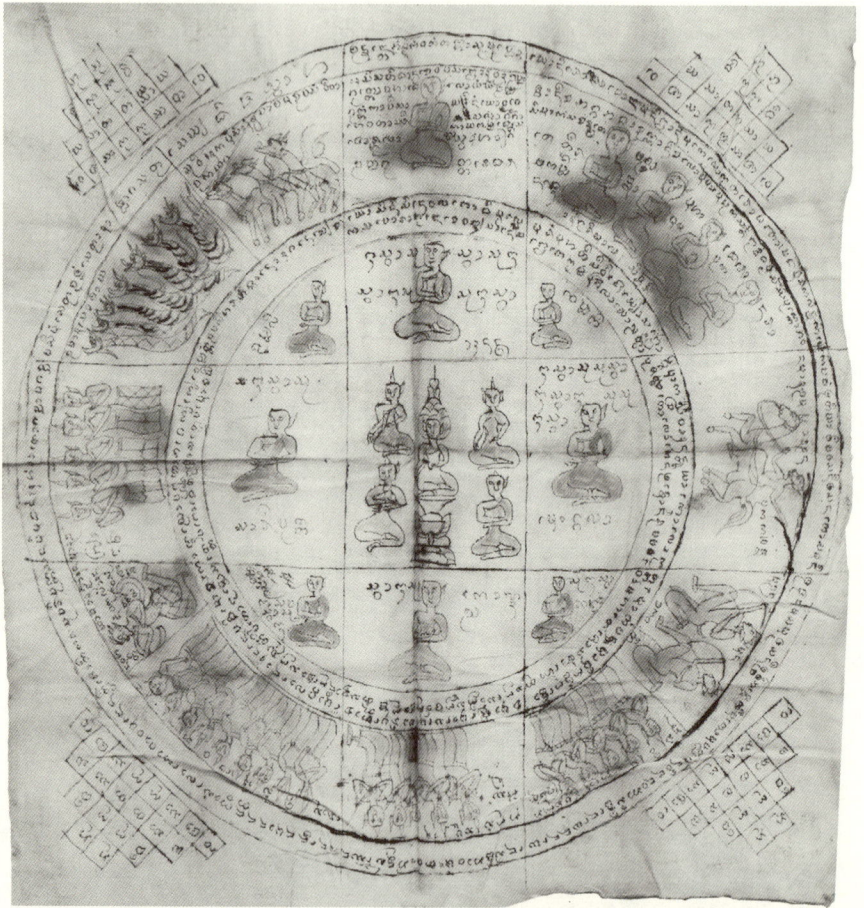

A Shan painted and printed cotton mandala illustrated with four past Buddhas and a Buddha of the future, private collection, Chiang Mai.

CHAPTER 3

NEGOTIATING WITH THE SPIRITS: TEXTS AND PRESCRIPTIONS

This chapter examines Pali incantations and magic spells (*katha*) used with magical images (*yantra*) and how astrology and cosmology feature in the process of creating them. Knowing the time when a person was born, the position of the planets and the phases of the moon are all essential information in calculating how an individual can be treated. Treatment will include a *yantra* and *katha* written in a variety of Tai, Burmese or Khmer script, some now no longer in use or understood.

When people consult a *saya* he asks for their day, month and year of birth, set according to the Buddhist Era or Shan Era calendar. The year 2553 of the Buddhist Era equates to 2104 of the Shan Era. The Lan Na year begins in September/October on the first day of the waxing moon and ends in August/September on the last day of the waning moon. The Shan year begins in November/December on the first day of the waxing moon and ends in September/October on the last day of the waning moon. The days of the week are counted one to seven beginning with Sunday or one to eight beginning with Sunday with Wednesday split from midnight to before noon and from noon to before midnight. The counting system used in this chapter is based on eight time periods.

Calculating according to eight time periods is a common divination tool. Each period is linked to the Sun, Moon, Mars, Mercury, Jupiter, Venus, Saturn and Rahu, matched to units of power called 'life force'. Those born on Sunday are one, matched to the sun and a life force of six. Those born on Monday are two, the moon and fifteen. Tuesday are three, Mars and a life force of eight. Wednesday from midnight to before noon are four, Mercury and seventeen. Wednesday in the afternoon or evening until midnight are five, Rahu and twelve. Thursday are six, Jupiter and a life force of nineteen. Friday are Venus, seven and twenty-one. Saturday are eight, Saturn and ten. The total units of life force add up to one hundred and eight that also symbolises the number of signs and symbols of the Buddha's footprint.

These life force numbers are an integral part in preparing *yantra* on mulberry paper. For example, if a patient was born on Saturday, the life force is ten. In that case, if a healing ritual is held for the patient, the number of strands plied together for each wick will number ten. These rolled wicks will be lit in ten bowls of oil and placed around the patient's bed while a healing *katha* that may include a reference to ten is chanted by the *saya*. When the wicks burn out, the ash deposit is collected from the ten bowls and mixed with vegetarian food and fed to the patient.

The eight time periods are also vital in calculations to establish whether a person is in an auspicious or inauspicious phase in life. A *yantra* of nine squares is drawn on a sheet of mulberry paper. Eight are filled with script while the central square is left vacant. Eight squares represent eight time periods and their corresponding life force. The top right-hand square represents Sunday, so six is written in the square. The square below is Monday, so fifteen is written in that square. This continues around until all eight life force numbers are in place. The *saya* begins by counting the square with the number representing the time period when the person was born. His counting proceeds clockwise for men and anticlockwise for women. The numbers of life force are added from square to square until a sum is reached, closest to the person's age. The time period in the square where the counting stops is compared with the starting square that is the time period when the person was born. If the *saya* calculates the numbers are compatible, the person is in an auspicious phase of life, and he predicts when that auspicious period will end. If he calculates the numbers are incompatible, it is an inauspicious phase and some kind of misfortune is predicted unless an appropriate *yantra* and *katha* are prepared and a ritual held to respect the Buddha and appease the spirits.

Complicated time period systems are not always necessary for divination. A villager can calculate auspicious periods himself, for example auspicious times to plant and harvest rice, to buy farm animals and make domestic decisions. He studies the phases of the moon visible to the naked eye. He charts the lunar cycle in chalk on a wall at home or buys a simple lunar chart in the market. The chart records eight phases of the moon with a sliding scale of dots (auspicious), crosses (inauspicious) and blank spaces (neutral) indicating power levels through each phase.[1] A full moon in November is particularly auspicious and marked with the highest number of dots.

However, villagers do consult *saya* when making major decisions in life, for example building a new house, getting married or planning a funeral. For housebuilding, a lunar chart is incorporated with the movements of a *naga*, the dragon spirit of the underworld. The *naga* moves through four lunar cycles matched to the four cardinal directions. The lunar cycle from February to May is auspicious when the head of the *naga* faces west, its tail east and its back north. The lunar period from May to August is inauspicious as the head of the *naga* faces north, the tail to the south and the back to the east. August to November is auspicious when the head faces east, the tail to the west and the back to the south. November to February is auspicious when the head faces south, the tail to the north and the back to the west. Once the most auspicious time is selected and matched to the birth data of the individual, the *saya* records on paper or cotton cloth the position of the *naga*, the phase of the moon, the day and time when building starts and the name and birth data of the owner of the new building. Hand- and footprints appear on some of the older housebuilding cloths, suggesting the owner might be illiterate and the prints were a substitute for a signature, but they may have been part of a ritual for good luck. Housebuilding records of this

---

1. The moon has nine phases but eight are counted; the ninth is defined as 'invisible'.

type were stored in the rafters of houses and treated as good luck talismans. Before the advent of a government land registry, they were the records.

The phases and power of the moon and sun also are not always recorded in *yantra* but feature in *katha*. Before the era of paved roads, Shan traders chanted *katha* for protection on their difficult journeys along jungle paths, over mountain passes and by fast-flowing rivers prone to floods. A *katha* recorded in Tai Yai (Shan) script includes, among other phrases, "I am the king of the moon" and "I am the king of the sun", both recited thirty-seven times at nightfall and at daybreak. Invoking the power of the sun and moon and repeating the entire *katha* thirty-seven times is a combined appeal to the power of the sun, moon and thirty-seven spirits of the Shan pantheon.

Scripts for *Yantra* and *Katha*

Saya writing *yantra* and *katha* are from among several Tai groups who have their own forms of script. At the time the manuscripts referenced in this book were written, Tai scripts were being used with smatterings of Khmer, considered a particularly powerful script, and Burmese script used for writing phrases in Pali. It is likely that monk scribes learnt powerful words and phrases for use in *katha* on their travels between monasteries. *Katha* were also circulated among village *saya* as it was not necessary to be literate to copy a few magical letters and numbers or learn to repeat them orally. Although many Tai scripts are now defunct, powerful letters and syllables, phrases and numbers continue in circulation.

Professor Sai Kham Mong describes one of the earliest Tai scripts as Hto Ngouk, meaning "letters like plant shoots".[2] The Tai living along the Burma-China border call it *lik kai khe*, "chicken scratchings". This term expresses well the appearance of long, uneven and backward-sloping letters.

---

2. Sai Kam Mong, *The History and Development of the Shan Scripts*, Chiang Mai: Silkworm Books, 2004, pp. 83–117.

There are sixteen consonants, six vowels and no tone marks. It was used for secular correspondence, and because of its expressive, exaggerated letters it was possible to create swirling amorphous shapes resembling ghosts and spirits. According to legend, a Tai prince sponsored monk scribes to standardise *lik kai khe* and add extra letters so that it could be used for writing Pali. The letters were given a rounded shape, more like Burmese script. Standardisation meant they lost fluidity for creating random magical images.[3]

Dua Tham is the general term for Tai script.[4] Tham Lan Na is an ancient script identified in fourteenth-century stone inscriptions and used to write Pali, and later for writing Lan Na dialect. Tai Khoen, Tai Yai and Tai Lue developed in other regions inhabited by the Tai.[5] They were probably created during a similar time frame. In terms of word construction, there are slight differences in spelling, but the underlying meaning is the same.[6] Dua Tham is written in regular horizontal lines from left to right or with letters stacked one above the other, a method used for creating outlines of weird amorphous spirits. Khom Mueang is the general term for written language used to address the spirits.

Phrases of Khmer script appear in *yantra* because Cambodian *saya* were reputed to write the most powerful spells. In the 1920s Khmer script was linked to claims of divinity by Ong Kammadon, a charismatic leader who led a rebellion against the French.[7] The messages he wrote in Khmer script were legendary for their mystical power. Khmer remains popular today

3. Informants from Shan States who recognise pre-reform Shan writing call it 'old Shan'.

4. William J. Hanna of Payap University, Chiang Mai helped with these identifications.

5. Ibid.

6. Gregory Kourilsky and Vincent Berment, 'Towards a Computerization of the Lao Tham System of Writing', paper presented at the First International Conference on Lao Studies, Northern Illinois University, Dekalb, 20–22 May 2005.

7. Tom Vater and Aroon Thaewchatturat, *Sacred Skin: Thailand's Spirit Tattoos*, Bangkok: Visionary World, 2011; René Drouyer, *Thai Magic Tattoos: The Art and Influence of Sak Yant*, Bangkok: River Books, 2013.

for writing tattoos.[8] Siamese script was introduced into Lan Na following political change in the late nineteenth and early twentieth century. It exists in manuscripts held in monastery libraries located in and around Chiang Mai where Siam first exerted influence.

Burmese script is characterised by regular circular and compact letters. It was introduced into Shan State probably during Burmese occupation in the sixteenth century and used for writing Pali incantations. When Tai Yai and Burmese script appear in the same formula, the Pali is written in Burmese script while magical language is in Tai script. An example is found in a protective talisman called the 'Five Buddha formula', four past Buddha and the Buddha of the future, represented in Burmese script, while the protective chant calling the spirits is Tai Yai script.[9]

When produced in *yantra*, Pali incantations are shortened. Words become individual letters or short syllables that fit inside squares, rectangles, circles and star shapes.[10] For example, the Pali phrase *cakkuma caramacinno, dhammannu dhammasamiko, balupetobaldharo* is reduced in a *yantra* to *ca, dha, dha* and *ba*. The phrase *Itipiso, svakkhato, supatipanno* is condensed to the letters *i* for *itipiso*, the syllable *sva* for *svakkhato* and *su* for *supatipanno*.[11] The chant *om* stands for *om mani padme hum*. There are some irregular shapes, too, for example *namo buddhaya* becomes a spiralling cone of two elongated letters *n* and *b* representing "Hail to the Buddha".[12]

A square *yantra* divided into fifty-six squares contains shorthand, the letters written in a grid accommodating the Pali text *Recollection of the*

8. B. J. Terwiel, *Monks and Magic: An Analysis of Religious Ceremonies in Central Thailand*, Bangkok: White Lotus, 1994, p. 50.

9. The Horniman Museum manuscript nn 12674, Horniman Museum collections, London.

10. Information provided by Phra Suphachai Chayasubho, Wat Suan Dork, Chiang Mai, 2011.

11. Catherine Becchetti, *Le mystère dans les lettres: étude sur les yantra bouddhiques du Cambodge et de la Thaïland*, Bangkok: Editions des cahiers de France, 1991, p. 4.

12. Interview with the monks of Wat Chieng Yin, Keng Tung, 2011.

Buddha.[13] The words *itipiso bhagava araham, samma-sambuddho vijja caranasampanno sugato, lokavidu, annuttaro purisa dammasalathi, sattha deva manussanam, Buddho, Bhagavati* are reduced to fifty-six letters and short syllables, placed in sequence to form diamond patterns.[14] A central star formation contains the final words of the text, *deva-manussanam Buddho Bhagavati* divided into *de, va, ma, nus, sa, nam, Bud, dho, Bha, ga, va* and *ti.*

Yantra reduced to shorthand is one way of accommodating a text in a diagram. The other is through coded letters and numbers. Secret codes enhance the magic power. When codes are used, individual letters are systematically removed from one word and repositioned in another, or written upside down or in mirror image, or split into syllables placed inside *yantra* in a pattern formation. This technique is described by *saya* as "dancing magic letters".[15] Symbols are used to indicate a particular ritual technique, for example exhaling breath over clients or ceremonial objects. Words and syllables can be formulated into phonic spells, for example the call of animals, a roaring tiger and the screech of a lucky lizard, or they can indicate spirits calling to this world or humans calling to the spirits. An example is the use of the phrase "Please come" to call the spirits back to the body in a healing ritual, written as a comma-shaped symbol in a *yantra*.[16] Copied on mulberry paper, the *yantra* is rolled with a cotton wick and a fragment of cloth once used to cover the face of a corpse. It is immersed in

---

13. The website of Phra Suphachai Chayasubho, Wat Suan Dork, Chiang Mai. borana@cmu.th

14. The full translation is "He is the Blessed One, a Worthy One with a mind free from defilements, the Perfectly Self-Awakened One, impeccable in knowledge and conduct, the accomplished one, knower of all worlds. He is well-being, going to a good destination, the Accomplished One, the Knower of the Worlds, the Supreme Teacher of those wishing to be taught, Teacher of the Divine and human beings, the Awakened one, Enlightened and Holy, the Blessed One."

15. Interview with Lung Ae Piya Wong, Mae Hong Son, 2008.

16. If a spirit leaves the body there are negative consequences, including physical and mental illness manifested in this case as nightmares.

a bowl of oil and set alight and the *katha* "Please come" is repeated as the wick burns.

Other square *yantra* contain shorthand letters and phrases placed in the squares to create distinct patterns. An example is a *yantra* containing an auspicious Abhidhamma text. It was produced for the dedication of a Buddhist monument. The *yantra* has twenty-five squares arranged in a five-by-five grid. Each contains a phrase from the *Abhidhamma Pitaka*.[17] If an imaginary line were drawn to link the phrases in sequence, a star shape emerges. The central square in the *yantra* is empty as it is the space where the name of the monument, the donors and the auspicious date of dedication are added. Diagrams of this type were also copied on cloth or incised in metal and lowered with other ritual offerings into the centre core of the monument by way of a special cavity. The text of the *Abhidhamma* as written on the *yantra* is chanted with other incantations during the dedication. The central core is then sealed.

Pali texts are prescribed in *yantra* that prevent nightmares, believed to be caused by evil spirits. A text to protect children who are thought to be particularly vulnerable is taken from the Pali *Ratana Sutta* that extolls the virtues of the Buddha, the *dhamma* and the *sangha*.[18] The words are written in shorthand on a sheet of mulberry paper, immersed in a bowl of water and placed on an altar in front of a Buddha image. The words of the *Ratana Sutta* are chanted, then the bowl is taken from the altar and laid in front of the door leading to the child's room.

Yantra with tier-shaped devotional/religious buildings (*prasad*) forming the illustration are frequently found in Tai manuscripts. They are prepared for candle rituals held by individual members of a congregation or a whole community seeking tolerance and loving-kindness (*metta*). This is

17. The *Abhidhamma Pitaka* is an analysis and summary of the Buddha's teachings in the sacred texts (*sutta*).

18. A Buddhist discourse in the Pali Canon.

an expensive undertaking as the beeswax to make a large candle is costly because it is sold by weight in local markets.[19] The *prasad* is drawn in a tier shape with each tier representing a plane of existence from the highest (*arupaloka*) to the lowest (*niraya*).[20] Although there are thirty-one planes in total, the number represented in *yantra* varies. Some focus on specific planes, for example sixteen for the realms of form (*rupaloka*), eleven for the realms of desire (*kamaloka*). Some *prasad* are decorative with tiered finials, pairs of rods and streamers to symbolise *metta* radiating outwards into the world. Inside the *prasad* are squares containing numbers that add up in total to the auspicious one hundred and eight that represents the one hundred and eight symbols of the Buddha's footprint and the one hundred and eight units of the life force.[21] Squares also accommodate shorthand letters and phrases for stanzas of the *Metta Sutta*.[22] A protective Pali text is transcribed on each side of the *prasad* and the names of sponsors, their families and associates are written at the base.

Yantra prepared for a community ritual when a large candle has been ordered are prepared to meet the size of the candle. Copied on a large sheet of mulberry paper or on cotton cloth, the *yantra* is folded according to prescribed instructions provided by a *saya*. It is bound to a cotton wick by an auspicious number of bindings also prescribed by the *saya*, then inserted inside the hollow candle that burns while stanzas of the *Metta Sutta* are chanted.

Other sources for creating *yantra* are drawn from planetary and natural forces. Planets are represented in *yantra* by numbers that relate to their life

19. For a ritual in Mae Hong Son, a group of Shan devotees paid one thousand and nine baht for the wax alone, December 2007.

20. Patricia Herbert, 'Burmese Cosmological Manuscripts', in *Burma: Art and Archaeology*, eds. Alexandra Green and T. Richard Blurton, London: British Museum Press, 2002, pp. 77–97.

21. Information provided by Noh Kham, Mae Hong Son, 2008.

22. *Metta* is one of the ten perfections of Buddhism. It promotes interpersonal harmony and meditative concentration.

force. For example, Jupiter is represented by the number nineteen, written in *yantra* as five, four, five, five. The moon is expressed as fifteen, divided into three fives or five threes, the sun as six in two threes and Saturn as two fives to make ten. The elements are reduced to short phrases, *ba* for earth and *ka* for fire. Powerful *yantra* containing these numbers and phrases are copied on mulberry paper and in one prescription are used to prevent nightmares when administered with a Pali incantation.

However, the numbers in *yantra* are not always related to planetary counting systems as described above but are auspicious numbers because a powerful *saya* has chosen them or they are universally known as lucky numbers. They are included with phrases and codes in *yantra*.[23] An example is a *yantra* that specifically treats a woman who has lost a child. A combination of lucky numbers is inscribed on copper and worn as a talisman to protect the woman from further loss. For women having difficulty in conceiving, a *yantra* of lucky numbers is copied on mulberry paper and nailed to a barren tree. If the tree blossoms and bears fruit, the same numbers are inscribed on metal and worn as a talisman. The instructions in the manuscript that recommends this treatment indicate that nailing the *yantra* to a tree is a test of efficacy.[24]

Letters and numbers in *yantra* are usually set and not altered although there are exceptions. Changes can reflect requests from individual clients, for example converting a general treatment for healing into one that treats a specific disease. Details of what can be changed are given in the manuscript. An example is found in the Horniman Museum used in illustrations in this book. It is a *yantra* laid out in squares and dissected by diagonal lines to form sets of triangles. Each triangle contains letters and phrases. Notes written to the side of the *yantra* give details of the circumstances in which the letters

23. Library of Congress collections.

24. Local farmers believe that hammering a nail in a barren tree is a stimulant to make it flower and fruit.

can be altered, although there is a caveat that no changes can be made to create negative power.[25]

Yantra formed in rectangles and circles can have parts left purposely empty, so they appear incomplete. Any missing parts are explained as *pong pheuw*. They represent a void that suffering and unhappiness can pass through.[26] An incomplete rectangular *yantra* of sixteen squares contains letters, lucky numbers and Pali phrases has five squares missing.[27] This *yantra* is inscribed on a plate of gold or silver and worn as a good luck talisman and prescribed as treatment to alleviate anxiety and suffering that with *katha* can be coaxed into the void. It is used as a treatment for women who have trouble conceiving a child and aims to remove their anxiety to create a calm state of mind that *saya* claim is key to achieving pregnancy.

Saya are called to write *yantra* to protect homes against evil spirits. This can involve four *yantra* to protect the cardinal directions. A *yantra* created for this purpose is a square or rectangular diagram containing Pali incantations and magic spells for protection. It is copied on mulberry paper that is bound around a cotton candle wick and inserted in a hollow beeswax candle. The *saya* carries the candle and tips it to allow the wax to drip on the floor in a defined space while chanting to prevent evil spirits from entering. Alternately, he may copy the *yantra* on four separate sheets of mulberry paper rolled around cotton wicks and immersed in four separate bowls of oil, set in the cardinal directions near the entrance to the house.[28] Magic spells and Pali incantations are offered while the wicks burn.

---

25. The Horniman Museum manuscript nn 12674.
26. Interview with the monks of Wat Chieng Yin, Keng Tung, 2011.
27. The Horniman Museum manuscript nn 12674, 152/65 (12).
28. Interview with the Ven. Sai Khemacari, Wat Chieng Yin, Keng Tung, 2011.

Magic Spells

Yantra are selected for rituals with accompanying magical spells (*katha*). Below is a list of *katha* translated from an old Tai Yai script by the Shan *saya* Long Te Za and Long Noi Na into modern Shan script. Khun Tun Yee, a local interpreter, translated from modern Shan into English.[29] Long Te Za and Long Noi Na listed physical and mental illnesses and the *katha* that cured them. The aim is to drive away evil spirits that cause illness and restore calm and balance to the body and mind. A *saya* chants over the patient while intoning the selected *katha*, or the words are written on mulberry paper, wrapped around a cotton wick and set alight in a bowl of oil. Or the mulberry paper is immersed in a bowl of water for a selected amount of time to allow the water to be charged with beneficial power. It is administered as a drink.

Katha Kya Ju Tham Pian gives general protection against evil spirits.

Katha Hya Kae Laed cures headaches and stomach disorders.

Katha Hya Tha Pang cures painful eye infections that cause redness and swelling.

Katha Thum Khong Pi Pur Pi Sur (*Hsa Pur*) exorcises ghosts that haunt the body and take control of the mind.

Katha Hya Ar Thad neutralises the harmful power of a potion administered by an inexperienced *saya*, for example medicine that contains an ingredient of ash collected after burning an incorrectly written *yantra* or cotton fabric printed with an incorrect *yantra* that was swallowed.

Katha Hya Thuk Mai Thuk Tham cures a fever and restores normal temperature to a person who is cold.

Katha Hya Khya provides a general cure for those in a poor state of health.

29. I am indebted to Khun Tun Yee from Mae Hong Son for interviewing the *saya* Long Tan Kyo Ho who was able to translate excerpts from spells and provide information on their use.

Katha Hya Sae Yo cures stomach problems.

Katha Hya Ai/Hsa Loam treats a persistent cough and sore throat.

Katha Mat Hsur provides protection against attack by wild animals in the jungle.

Katha Hya Tong Jiep cures illnesses of the digestive tract.

Katha Hya Tha Wod Jiep cures painful eye ailments and blindness caused by a lack of treatment.

Katha Nae Hya Lerd Haeng treats blood clots and stops haemorrhaging.

Katha Kon Kwang Lerd Yong Lerd Wa is part of the cure for mental disorders and insanity (translated as 'mad and crazy').

Katha Kon Yo Lerd Yu cures people who are anaemic and have developed a skin disease.

Katha Hya Ngan treats the body in a state of shock resulting from a fever.

Katha Hya Khaeng Dai Pak cures paralysis of the body and brings feeling back to limbs.

Katha Hya Loam Lu (Loam Kheun) treats general ill health, high blood pressure and painful skin lesions.

Katha Pong Hsam Tha provides help to remember events from the past and to predict the future.

Katha Hya Khya Na cures skin abnormalities and infections on the face and body.

Katha Hya Kae Nao is a general cure for illness.

Katha Muk Ka La Long helps predict the future and ensure success in life.

Katha Tham Pian protects against ghosts and evil spirits appearing in dreams. The person fears the apparitions will come alive to haunt them.

Katha Hya Long Hsa Kyam is an all-encompassing power to cure evil.

Katha Hya Pi Pur (Teuk Pur) protects the body and mind against evil ghosts and spirits that try to control them.

Katha Teuk Pi resists the power of ghosts and evil spirits.

Katha Hya Ma Hyo treats women who suffer from menstrual pain and haemorrhage.

Katha Nae Hya Tham cures painful flesh wounds caused by cuts from a
   sharp weapon.

Katha Hya Theuk Ka La treats people with undiagnosed symptoms.

Katha Hya Tha Jiep cures painful red eyes.

Katha Hya Lerd Lu cures anaemia and resulting dry skin.

Katha Hya Tha Pae Tha Mo cures tired, itchy eyes.

Katha Hya Nuk Khong treats a seriously ill patient who is close to death.

Katha Hya Ho Khai cures headaches and dizziness.

Katha Hya Tha Pae Tha Pang treats eye diseases and blindness.

Ka Ta Sya Kae Na protects travellers wherever they go.

Katha Nae Hya Song Hon cures vomiting and illnesses of the digestive tract.

Katha Hya Tha Pae cures eye complaints.

Katha hya nuk khong is given to a patient as a treatment of last resort. The
   words are copied on four separate sheets of mulberry paper, bound
   with cotton wicks and immersed in four shallow bowls of vegetable oil,
   placed at the head, feet and on each side of the patient who is laid with
   the head pointing towards the east. The wicks are lit and *katha* chanted.
   The ash deposit from the burning wicks is collected and removed far
   away from the patient to a site specified by a *saya*. The removal of the
   ash signifies evil spirits being exorcised.

Katha mat hsur provides protection for long-distance travellers subject to
   tropical diseases, bandit raids and attacks by wild animals. The words
   create an invisible defence against an aggressor, chanted repeatedly
   while stroking the surface of a protective body tattoo.

Katha nae hya tham protects a traveller against attack by wild animals.

Katha ma ha ni yom ensures a jury will reach a 'not guilty' verdict however
   damning the evidence against the accused. The words are copied on
   mulberry paper and soaked in water for a prescribed time. The power
   of the *katha* is absorbed in the water. The accused washes his face in the
   water as an act of purification. The jury declares him innocent.

Katha ma ha ni yom secures a guilty verdict on someone who is innocent. The *katha* is copied on mulberry paper. The name of the innocent party and their birth data are added. Evil spirits are called on to magically influence the jury to convict.

Katha hya ar tat neutralises a harmful formula administered to a victim. The word *tat* means to 'put a stop' to evil. The *katha* is copied on a sheet of mulberry paper, bound with a cotton wick and immersed in a shallow dish of oil. The words of the *katha* are chanted while the wick burns. The ash is collected, diluted in water and taken as a drink. Several days are allowed to pass before the *saya* is confident the victim has recovered, and his body and mind have stabilised.

Dealing with Evil Spirits, Witches and Ghosts

This chapter has shown how supernatural forces are mobilised to improve lives using positive *yantra* and *katha*. In contrast, dealing with evil spirits, witches and ghosts is the work of *maw paeng*. It involves complicated recipes with ingredients that include plants, trees, animal extracts, insects and human and animal bones. These ingredients are often mixed with fragments and shavings taken from objects that are specifically Buddhist, for example chips taken from a monk's bowl. However, the Buddhist materials used in these prescriptions are probably viewed as unclean, such as shavings from a mud-stained monastery ladder or mud from the hem of a monk's robe. It is likely such substances were stolen from a monastery specifically to be used in black magic, the act of stealing itself evil, adding to the overall power of a polluted prescription.

Maw paeng harness the power of natural objects struck by the forces of nature, for example bark from trees and the bones of animals struck by lightning. *Maw paeng* also exploit human tragedies by using the bones from corpses of murder victims, and manipulate angry spirits released from the bodies of victims of violent crime. They include in the ingredients disease-carrying insects like flies and cockroaches. *Maw paeng* can use their skills to magically introduce polluted substances into the body of a victim, causing mental and physical illness. Although the focus of their work is on creating evil, there is one positive role as *maw paeng* can manipulate evil spirits to identify criminals.

Maw paeng operate within a code. The potential victim must be an evil person who deserves to suffer. Permitted targets are those who cause serious physical and mental harm to their victims as well as those who damage or destroy the property of others on at least three occasions. Those who live honest lives and observe at least five Buddhist precepts are not victimised. If an innocent person of high moral standing is victimised in error, that person will suffer no ill effects because Buddhism will protect them. However, this code operates according to the Buddhist lore of *karma*. Those who live blameless lives in this life cycle may be targeted if they committed serious offences in a previous life.

Prescriptions

Prescription can banish evil spirits, prevent evil acts by human witches and neutralise the malign power of ghosts. One involves scrapings from residue on a wooden cooking ladle used in the upper part of a rice steamer. Shavings ranging from a wooden house pillar, house door and house ladder to those from a wooden house ladder and door leading to a monastery building are added with seven rice grains from wastewater residue collected under a dish-washing shelf and seven green-headed flies. These ingredients are grated and ground together into a powder. This prescription – weigh 816.465 milligrams of the powder and add shavings from a banana tree trunk, then wrap in a banana leaf and grill over a fire – is used to cure a fever and body aches caused by evil spirits, witches or ghosts.

The above prescription can also stop contract killers, witches and ghosts from committing the murder of a potential victim. The intended victim sits on a worn mat on the floor facing the east. He holds in his hands an old, chipped bowl made in the Shan State of Mong Kueng filled with the ground ingredients from the previous prescription. The amount in the bowl is weighed to match the number of assassins. One assassin will be deterred by the weight equivalent to one rosemary pea seed (272.155 milligrams). Two assassins are deterred by the weight of two rosemary pea seeds. For three assassins, the weight is three rosemary pea seeds (816.365 milligrams).

The following recipe gives ingredients for exterminating evil spirits and ghosts. Grind together nutmeg, cloves, five *umbelliferae* (fennel, anise or sweet fennel, cumin, black cumin, dill), pepper, asafoetida, opium, wild ginger, sweet flag and small rhizome ginger. Add seven ground cockroaches, seven shredded spiders' skins, seven shredded horse fly skins and seven rice grains of leftover rice collected from a crack in a wooden mortar. Mix in seven shavings from the outer strut of a wooden house ladder, a hair from the heads of three village headmen and three widows and shavings from the bone of a human corpse. Collect some charcoal residue from a cremation site, shavings from a wooden pole used to turn burning corpses during cremation, soil from a graveyard and alfalfa grass growing by a graveyard. Add thirty-three scrapings from a tree root growing across a village path, thirty-three scrapings from a tree stump by a village path, thousands of different flowers [sic], thirty-three shoots from different trees [sic], thirty-three pieces of plant roots growing in water and wood from three trees struck by lightning. This powerful recipe can only be prepared on Tuesdays and Saturdays.

The next two prescriptions deal with possession, the first to cure a person possessed by an evil spirit or witch. Grind to a powder the shavings of burnt wood from a funeral pyre, sweet flag, thorn apple, Indian ivy rue, pepper and dog bush. Dilute the powder in water and take as a drink. Or mix the powder with oil and use as a body rub. The second prescription is for injection. To treat a person possessed by a witch, grind together seven seeds of Indian or Jamaican wild liquorice, seven long pepper corns, seven regular pepper corns, seven slices of wild ginger, seven slices of small turmeric, seven slices of small rhizome ginger and shavings from the trunk of a fishtail palm. Add 1.02058 grams of yellow cinnabar and seven slices of sweet flag. Sieve the mixture and add lime juice. Administer as an injection under the skin.

Hungry Ghosts and Cannibal Spirits

There are many prescriptions for dealing with hungry ghosts that possess humans. Hungry ghosts are particularly frightening as they have massive appetites and drive those they possess to madness. Grind to a powder seven shredded bed bug skins, seven shredded spider skins, earth taken from seven steps of a wooden house ladder and three pieces of stick lac growing on wood or bamboo under the roof of a house. Dilute in warm water and take as a drink. Another prescription is used as a skin rub. Grind together 1,088.62 milligrams of arsenic trisulphide, 1,088.62 milligrams of Ridley's staghorn fern and four seeds of white rosary pea or four seeds of Indian wild liquorice. Mix the powder with oil and apply as a body rub.

A complex prescription to expunge ghosts and witches includes a wide range of ingredients, including objects, humans and animals struck by lightning. Grind together black leadwort, rosy leadwort, white leadwort, Ceylon oak, blackberry lily or candy lily, pepper, money plant or devil's ivy, giant fern tree, cardamom and sweet flag. Add ground bone from a human killed by lightning and wood from a tree struck by lightning. Add extract from a tiger's head, ground bone and horn from a white buffalo struck by lightning, ground bone from a human who died in violent circumstances, ground bone from a python, a black dog, a black chicken, a crow and a black cat and a skin shed by a snake. Add soft earth collected from the middle of a pathway in the forest, a hornet taken from a hornet's nest close to a graveyard and a piece of crushed tile taken from the floor close to a Buddha image. Add earth from a pig stye, mud from the hem of a monk's robe, mud from a door and mud from a baby's shirt. Mix with seven whole rice grains taken from the bottom of a mortar, seven cracked rice grains, seven shredded spider skins, seven thin bamboo strips, the tail of a long-tailed king crow and the tail of a falcon. Add mud from a nest of the dauber wasp, chippings from a cracked pot found at the shrine of the town guardian spirit and chips from a cracked alms bowl found in the ordination hall of a Buddhist monastery. Add a dung beetle, green flies, a centipede, a bumblebee, a cockroach and a few winged termites. Grind all the ingredients together to a powder and place in a bamboo basket. Leave the basket at a place far away from the victim. Call the evil spirits using *katha* led by a *maw paeng*. Chant a Buddhist religious text (*sutta*) at home for three nights to ward off any further harm.

Cannibal spirits are seen as more terrifying than hungry ghosts. To drive away a cannibal spirit, grind to a powder a stick of firewood, shavings from a tree struck by lightning, earth and human ashes from a graveyard, rabbit droppings, wild ginger, yellow turmeric, white turmeric root, asafoetida and water pepper. Dilute the powder in warm water and take as a drink.

Maw paeng can be asked to use their negative power in a positive way, for example using certain *katha* to appeal to evil spirits to help identify an evil person who has caused harm to an innocent victim. Or they can be asked to identify a robber by using the words of a spell copied on a strip of mulberry paper nailed to a wall close to where the robbery took place. The *maw paeng* chants a *katha* seven times a day for seven days and by the last day will receive a message from the spirits identifying the thief.

Although most *maw paeng* can administer prescriptions and control evil spirits, witches and ghosts, there are instances where control is lost, causing mayhem in society. There may be mental instability. Drunken and disorderly men harass monks, desecrate graves and engage in vicious fights. *Maw paeng* exhaust all possibile ways of dealing with wayward spirits and so seek help by reciting Buddhist *sutta* and Pali incantations praising the Attributes of the Buddha, the Eightfold Path and the Triple Gem. A *maw paeng* may decide to consult another *maw paeng* who has experience of exorcism. If all attempts fail, the *maw paeng* goes for help to a devout monk whose source of power is self-discipline and strict observance of many Buddhist precepts.

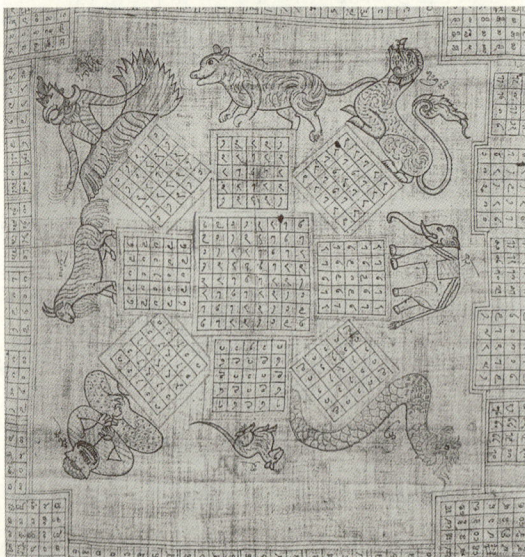

(*top*) Painted and printed cotton divination chart. This version has a *singha* opposite a primitive-looking female elephant, a male elephant opposite an ambiguous looking animal, Shan, nineteenth century. (De Siam Antiques) (*below*) Painted and printed cotton divination chart. In this version a *naga* is opposite a *garuda*, a monkey opposite a *singha*, a *phoo* (small Shan animal like a guinea pig) opposite a mouse and a male elephant opposite a goat, Shan, nineteenth century. (De Siam Antiques)

CHAPTER 4

TEXTILES AND CLOTHING

This chapter focuses on painted and printed textiles that bring to life in black and white and colour visions of the Tai supernatural world. In this magico-religious sphere of good and evil spirits, artists portray cosmological and astrological landscapes and the spirits that inhabit them. Textiles provide focus for meditation at home and in Buddhist monasteries, usually in the form of banners, a visual reminder of a world beyond human experience. Many are printed with texts and visual images, for example a text that contains protective words from a *paritta* recited to ward off misfortune, or a text for healing, not only in a physical sense but psychological healing through meditation by concentrating on a textile that portrays a calm, ordered world.

Some magical textiles are illustrated with propitious mascots and accompanying lucky numbers to bring success in commerce and the professions. These textiles may be quite small, the size of a handkerchief, kept in a pocket or concealed in the folds of a turban. Cloth was also used during wartime for drawing up plans of troop formations and military strategies and to record the position of the planets and stars to ensure battle began at an auspicious period. Rituals where cloth is treated as a ceremonial object and the means by which cloth acquires power are also included in this chapter.

Textiles are imbued with protective power when they feature *yantra* consisting of Buddhist iconography, mythical animals and spirits and magical diagrams, empowered with magic spells (*katha*). Protective turbans, shirts and jackets are empowered in this way. *Saya* carried bags printed with protective symbols for their ritual objects, inks and tattooing needles. If a bag was lined with a fragment of a monk's robe, protective power was increased. These unique and at times bizarre images on cloth were created by *saya* who chanted Buddhist incantations and magic spells during the creative process. They were most inspired during auspicious periods of time set according to a lunar calendar. But creating images and drawing magic spells was not the only way that cloth gained magical power. It could be absorbed through physical contact with a charismatic person, for example a revered abbott. After his death, his robes and other humble possessions continue to radiate goodness. The robes were distributed to the faithful as talismans. The funeral cloth that covered his face and body was paticularly potent (see Chapter 3).

The content of this art form is selective in its choice of imagery, often simplified forms of complex Buddhist cosmology. The anthropologist Stanley Jeyaraja Tambiah argued that most villagers did not understand complicated world systems and planes of existence within Buddhist cosmology.[1] In their sermons monks explain the fundamentals of Buddhist cosmology to their congregations, for example the world of *kamaloka* with its heavens of the lesser gods, as well as the world of men, demons, ghosts and animals. These are the figures illustrated in textile paintings as visions of the world that could be understood by the majority of people.

Set among painted and printed images are Pali incantations and magic spells written in a variety of Tai scripts and in Burmese and Khmer. Monks and educated lay people regard many of these textiles as containing 'incorrect' Pali. It is possible to argue that textual inaccuracy reflects the educational levels of the artists of the time who were simplifying Buddhist cosmology and astrology as the monks did in their sermons. Their expressive

1. Stanley Jeyaraja Tambiah, *Buddhism and the Spirit Cults in North-east Thailand*, Cambridge: Cambridge University Press, 1970.

landscapes and magical diagrams were capable of inspiring the faithful and were an excellent visual prop for meditation.

Although this chapter is concerned primarily with printed and painted cloth, handspun cotton thread is an essential component in Buddhist and spirit rituals. When tied around the wrists, cotton thread symbolises the attachment of body to spirit, and when used to close off a physical space it becomes a protective cordon for ritual participants. The Tai chronicles describe protection rituals held in Chiang Mai when cotton thread was used to enclose the entire city. In the past, rituals of this type were held following a defeat in battle, a disease epidemic or a severe drought leading to famine.[2] When woven using a macramé technique, cotton thread becomes a protective canopy. The number of filaments in the thread is ritually significant,[3] for example, using three-plied thread to represent the Triple Gem – the Buddha, the *sangha* (monks) and the *dhamma* (law) – and six plies to represent the life force of the sun. Plied cotton was handmade by village women and certain taboos governed the process. Only a select group of women beyond childbearing age were eligible.[4] This custom ended and today most plied cotton thread for ritual use is produced commercially.

These textiles have images that are painted and printed on the surface of cloth. This is in contrast to most textiles in inland Southeast Asia where patterns and images are introduced in the warp and weft threads on a loom, or the warp is a plain colour and the weft threads contain the patterns. There are exceptions, such as weavers in Loei Province, north Thailand who weave ghosts (*phi ta khon*) in weft patterns.[5] But painting and drawing in freehand

2. In 1991 the ritual was held in Chiang Mai following several catastrophic events, including the death of a revered monk and a series of fatal incidents, such as a plane crash that killed senior officials and dignitaries.

3. Plying means twisting cotton filaments together.

4. Susan Conway, *Thai Textiles*, London: British Museum Press, 1992, pp. 61–65.

5. Susan Conway, *HRH Maha Chakri Sirindhorn Textile Collection: Symbols of Love and Respect*, Bangkok: Office of HRH Princess Sirindhorn. Bangkok and Amarin Printing and Publishing Public Co. Ltd, 2020, pp. 76–77.

produces images without the restrictions imposed by the structure of a loom. It allows for individual style. Painting on cotton requires a smooth surface produced by sizing with rice paste mixed with a little saffron oil. When dry the surface is burnished with a stone. Black ink is made from soot mixed with animal bile or tree gum and is used for outlines, applied with a bamboo or quill pen. Until the advent of cheap commercial paints, colours were made from local pigments and applied with animal-hair brushes.[6] A few colours, like cobalt, were sometimes available in local markets.

Buddhism and the Spirits

An artist produces images of deities, planets, mythical landscapes, monks and humans and good and evil spirits. The Buddha and his followers feature prominently. The god Indra from the Buddhist pantheon is a major protector of Buddhism and is portrayed with his mount Erawan. Popular spirits include the lucky monk Phra Siwali, Phra Malai, an emissary between heaven and hell, and Phra Upakut, a princely water spirit. Because this is a world where farming and hunting were the main livelihoods, ploughs and farming tools appear alongside hunting bows and arrows. The annual cycle of rice planting coincides with Buddhist festivals, and villagers are portrayed enjoying festivities with music and dancing. Circling around and among these images are astrological symbols, Pali incantations and texts in local dialects.

Phra Upakut

In this world of humans and spirits, characters can transition from one world to another. Phra Upakut (Upagutta) is an example. He lives with the *naga* in the waters of the underworld and according to legend was an immaculate conception, the son of a Buddha, born by a mermaid

6. A list of local dyes and pigments is listed in Conway, *Thai Textiles*, p. 70.

and imbued with supernatural power. Phra Upakut comes up from the underworld when called, specifically to ward off evil spirits while the harvest festival of Bun Phrawees is held. He takes on the guise of a monk. The festival takes place every year in the dry season after the rice crop is harvested. Painted textile banners hung during this festival illustrate the magical transformation of Phra Upakut from water spirit to monk. The Bun Phrawees festival has two themes, thanksgiving for the harvest and a call for rain in preparation for the next agricultural cycle.[7] As a spirit of the watery underworld, Phra Upakut has power to bring monsoon rain.

It is the custom to formally request the presence of Phra Upakut by calling him from the underworld, a ritual performed by monks, elders, a *saya* and attendants. They bring a tray bearing a monk's bowl, a set of monk's robes, an umbrella and sandals in recognition of Phra Upakut's transformation. An image of the Buddha, fresh flowers, puffed rice, cigarettes and a water jug are also borne on a tray. The monks and *saya* go in procession, followed by villagers, to a riverbank, a pond or the shores of a lake where the monks offer incantations to summon Phra Upakut to the festival.[8] The *saya* calls on the spirits to look favourably on the festival and ensure a successful monsoon.

After the calling, the procession returns to the village monastery carrying a stone collected from the site. It is placed on the altar with the robes and offerings. Cloth banners portraying Phra Upakut are hung on the walls. As the monk's robes indicate, if he appears it will be as a monk who accompanies local monks when they collect alms in the early morning before the festival begins. According to legend, members of the lay community who give alms to Phra Upakut while unaware of his true identity gain religious merit and personal good fortune.

The ritual of thanksgiving during the Bun Phrawees festival involves reading one thousand verses of the *Vessantara Jataka*, the story of the

7. Tambiah, *Buddhism and the Spirit Cults in North-east Thailand*, pp. 152–75.
8. Phra Upakut is addressed in local dialect.

Buddha in his last life as a *bodhisattva*. It is read by members of the congregation.[9] The festival ends with thanksgiving by the monks and a prayer for good fortune and monsoon rain for the next season. Phra Upakut has successfully guarded the ritual and he will now return to the underworld. The stone that represented him is removed from the altar and taken back to the watery place where it was collected. The painted banner portraying Phra Upakut is taken down.

Painted cotton textiles displayed during the Bun Phrawees festival portray Phra Upakut as monk and a water spirit. In one finely painted banner he sits cross-legged on the rim of an octagon. Four images represent Phra Upakut as a princely water spirit wearing court dress, a golden headdress, a jacket trimmed with gold and a loincloth. He sits with hands joined in prayer, clasping lotus buds. The other four show Phra Upakut as a young monk dressed in saffron robes and holding a begging bowl. Eight fork-tailed lizards set between the figures denote good luck associated with him. The short texts written by the lizards' mouths are phonic spells, renditions of the lucky sound lizards make when calling. At the centre of the cloth are cosmic diagrams with letters and numbers set in squares, codes related to the eight time periods and units of cosmic force (see Chapter 3). A Pali text for protection is written around the edge of the cloth.

A Mandala

The basic principles of Buddhism are represented in the circles of a mandala, an important symbol for Buddhists throughout Asia. In structure the mandala has a core (*manda*) and enclosed circular elements (*-la*). It is a symbol of the *dharmachakra*, the Wheel of Law and endless cycles of rebirth. It symbolises an orderly cosmos with gods, humans, spirits, demons, ghosts and animals set around a central core containing the Buddha and

---

9. The reading takes nine to fourteen hours. It is often supplemented with other Buddhist texts, so the complete ritual can take up to two days.

his followers. In their iconography and ritual use, Tai mandalas represent aspects of the belief system, including Theravada Buddhism, good and evil spirits, astrology, cosmology and numerology.

At the centre of the mandala is an image of the Buddha, representing order and moral discipline. Concentric circles of Buddha images, monks, *arahat* (perfected persons) and spirit guardians surround and support the Buddha. Mythical warriors, ghosts, humans and animals occupy the outer circles of this enclosed space. Lines projecting outwards from the centre of the mandala represent spokes of wisdom.[10] Beyond the outer rim are representations of nature and cosmic forces. There are regional variations in style and proficiency as figures and landscapes reveal the vision of individual Tai artists. Although there is conformity in the stance of the Buddha and his followers, particularly in gestures (*mudra*) and dress, the outer circles of humans, spirits, demons and ghosts are imaginative and varied in their costume and the gestures they adopt. The most skilled religious painting is associated with important religious centres like Keng Tung, Chiang Saen and Chiang Mai where famous Buddha images were cast and were frequently copied in sculpture and paintings. Away from these main centres, artists worked in a provincial style.

There are rules governing the order in which an artist creates a mandala. He begins by drawing a Buddha image at the centre of the cloth on a day calculated to be auspicious. On subsequent auspicious days, figures around the Buddha are added. Monks claim that by working in this way a mandala can take up to a year to complete.[11] After ritual blessing, the mandala becomes a sacred object. With its theme of moral discipline and order it is considered an appropriate gift presented by monks to laymen, particularly those in authority, in the belief that they will meditate on the discipline of

10. Karen Armstrong, *Buddha*, UK: Viking Penguin, 2001.

11. The following three samples were produced in this way and are dated from the early to mid-nineteenth century.

the Buddha, his wisdom, compassion, fortitude and patience, and follow his example.[12]

Three mandalas are illustrated here. They were chosen to show how substance and style could vary. The first example is in Lan Na style. The emphasis is on healing and protection. The central Buddha is in the style of Chiang Saen, an ancient Lan Na city. Buddha images were produced in Chiang Saen from the tenth century and continuously copied.[13] This version is based on a Phra Singh Luang image from the late Chiang Saen period, dated to the fifteenth century.[14] Significantly, a Phra Singh Luang Buddha is renowned for miraculous healing power. The Buddha is seated in the emblematic *bhumisparsha mudra*. The writing is a *paritta*, and magical incantations are written in Tham Lan Na and Tai Khoen script. The figures encircling the Buddha are identified in an accompanying script as Maha Kasabha, Anarohta, Patiya, Analota, Juntha, Sujatha, Upakut (described above) and Rahula, son of Prince Siddhartha. The presence of Sujatha and Maha Kasabha is significant because their names are chanted in rituals to cure the sick.

The outer circle of the mandala contains nine Brahma, nine hungry ghosts, three spirits living in heaven, two spirits on horseback, nine *deva*, the spirit *yakka wasulo* wielding a club, and a thunderbolt (identified as Punnaka from the *Vidhurapandita Jataka*) and a group of mythological animals. The rim of the mandala contains the words of a *paritta*. Situated outside the circle at each of the four corners of the cloth are guardians of the cardinal directions (*thao thang si*) contained within enclosures shaped like lotus buds. The guardians are Virurakkha deva and Virupakka deva, guardians of the south and west, respectively, Kuvera, guardian of the north and Tatharattha, guardian of the east. Magic diagrams on each side

12. Information provided by the monks of Wat Chong Klang, Mae Hong Son, 2010.

13. Sarassawadee Ongsakul, *History of Lan Na*, Chiang Mai: Silkworm Books, 2005, p. 26.

14. The image is now in the temple of Wat Phra Singh, Chiang Mai.

are bordered by *naga* with their tails in their mouths. *Naga* adopt this position to symbolise an unbroken circle of good luck that bad luck cannot penetrate.[15] Horse-drawn chariots shaped like birds pull the sun, represented by a peacock, and the moon by a hare. The demon god Rahu, a good luck symbol in Lan Na and Shan mythology, is portrayed with tattooed arms holding a sphere representing the moon.[16]

The second mandala is in Shan style. Although in a similar format, there are differences in content and the way characters are portrayed.[17] A Shan-style Buddha seated in the *bhumisparsha mudra* is at the centre in a flame-like structure with lotus buds, a fan and a begging bowl. A *paritta* text written in Burmese script surrounds him. A circle of monks are seated in *bhumisparsha mudra* or kneeling in prayer with a spirit dressed in the style of a Shan prince. A Pali text encircles them. The outer circle of the mandala has kneeling monks and spirit guardians seated, dancing and on horseback. Among the group of mythological animals are nine *makara* who act as emissaries between earth and the realm of the gods.[18] A ring of Pali text in Burmese script is on the outer rim. Seated on the rim are four guardians of the cardinal directions, large imposing figures who ressemble warrior princes. They hold crossbows and tipped arrows, pairs of crossed swords and large clubs. Shan military drums (*kong loang*) are positioned between their legs. A set of four square and tiered diagrams separate them, topped with spiralling *unnalom* to signify *om*, an abbreviation of the mantra *om mani padme hum*. Outside the mandala is a colourful Buddhist landscape

15. Information provided by the monks at Wat Chong Klang, Mae Hong Son, 2010.

16. Rahu swallows the sun and moon to cause eclipses but is forced to release them by the power of an incantation referencing the Buddha. The stanza is incorporated in Buddhist liturgy as a paritta, recited by monks in prayers for protection.

17. Information provided by Sirot Chutiwat, Hang Dong, Chiang Mai Province, March 2013.

18. A *makara* is a mythological creature with the head of an elephant and the body of a scaled dragon.

with cloud-shaped boulders. The sun and moon are prominent, the sun as a peacock in a circle of red, the moon as a hare in a star-shaped firmament.

The third mandala is for meditating on the teachings of the Buddha. The way the figures are presented suggests it is the work of a less experienced artist. The colours are restricted to black and red that has bled from the figures. At the centre of the mandala are five Buddha images. Four are Buddhas of this era while the fifth is Maitreya, the Buddha of the future. One Buddha is seated in *dhyana mudra*, a gesture signifying meditation, tranquillity and the attainment of spiritual perfection. Three are in *bhumisparsha mudra*, the gesture of enlightenment. The fifth is in *dharmachakra mudra*, symbolising the Buddha's first sermon. Eight monks are positioned around the five Buddha images all seated in *dhyana mudra*. A circle of Pali text surrounds them. The outer circle of the mandala is divided into sections containing rows of monks seated in *dhyana mudra*, spirit guardians and warriors, *naga*, horses and rows of mythological animals. A circle of Pali text in Burmese and Tai Yai script encircles the outer rim. In place of guardian spirits, landscape and planets as in the previous samples, there are four stepped diagrams containing protective incantations.

In contrast to the circular form of the mandala, the cosmos can be represented in a vertical format with interpretations of *kamaloka* pared down to fit into this different structure. In the first sample illustrated here, the Buddha is seated at the summit of a vertical stem with eight branches bearing eight *bodhisattva* in *bhumisparsha mudra*, offspring of the Buddha's wisdom and compassion. Textiles on the theme of wisdom and compassion became significant in times of crisis, for example during war, famine or outbreaks of disease. The eight *bodhisattva* emphasise this theme. Akashagarbha represents purity, Avalokiteshvara compassion, Kshitigarbha merit, Maitreya activity, Manjushri wisdom, Samantabhadra prayer and offerings, Sarvanivarana-Vishkambhin purity and Vajrapani mystical power. The Pali incantation *araham, sammasam Buddha, sugato, lokavidu, anuttaro purisa dammasrathi, satthadeva manussanam, buddho, bhagava* becomes an incantation for protection. Set below the *bodhisattva* is an ocean with stylised waves full of sea snakes, fish and turtles. The spirit *yakka wasulo* holds the base of the vertical stem at the level of the waves. The text includes protective incantations and for loving kindness (*pi yam*).

In another version the vertical stem is replaced by a tall pillar with the Buddha positioned at the top of a world of monks, humans and spirits. A hare and peacock represent the sun and moon and a *makara* acts as an emissary between man and the realm of the gods. Good fortune in everyday life is symbolised by farming and hunting tools, weighing scales for trading and figures dancing to represent the pleasure enjoyed at festivals. Below is a watery underworld where animals, snakes, fish, crabs and *naga* dwell. A large fish is dormant in the water, known in legend as the 'earthquake fish'. The fish actually exists in the oceans of Southeast Asia. The myth is that if caught by a fisherman it is an omen of an impending earthquake with a disastrous tsunami to follow. The illustration suggests that in his position high on a pillar above the fish the Buddha is able to control it and prevent earthquakes and tsumanis from happening.

Although in many textile paintings there are multiple images on one cloth, samples exist with one image that acts as a focal point for meditation. Some are given added meaning by the inclusion of sets of auspicious numbers. The first sample illustrated here is for meditation and features a Lan Na-style Buddha seated in *bhumisparsha mudra* with stylised flowers, confined within a diamond-shaped frame. A Pali text paying respect to the Buddha is written in Tham Lan Na script.[19] Along the border are the numbers one to nine. Nine represents the nine levels of consciousness in human life. Five levels are the senses of touch, taste, sight, hearing and smell. The sixth level is learning that comes with full use of the five senses. The seventh level is without sensory perception, abstract, spiritual thoughts. The eighth level is karmic energy through interaction with others and the ability to understand

19. They resemble floral designs in Lan Na temple woodcarvings and metalwork.

the cause and effect of one's actions. The ninth level is a source of energy and mental and spiritual activity. In this textile the number five is repeated along the edge of the cloth to represent the Five Precepts: no taking of life, no stealing, no sexual misconduct, no falsehoods and abstaining from alcohol.

The second textile is based on the theme of loving-kindness (*metta*) and the illustration is erotic. At the centre of the cloth drawn in red ink is an image of a woman having sexual intercourse with a horse. This is not without precedent as mating with animals is part of spirit mythology and there are references in the *Bhurridata Jataka* to women mating with *naga*. The story behind the image of the woman and horse is of a loving husband who dies and is reborn as a horse. In his new equine form he searches for his wife, and when he finds her their love continues, expressed in this version as sexual intercourse.[20] An extensive text reinforces the moral theme of *metta* underlying the story, with Pali incantations based on the theme of loving-kindness and stanzas from the *Metta Sutta,* a text defining the qualities needed to achieve *metta.* This particular illustration comes in other forms, such as a woman with a husband reborn as a *naga* or an elephant.

The third textile is intended as a talisman for good luck in business. The central character is Nang Kwak, a female spirit whose reputation rests on an ability to lure customers into stores. Textiles with this image were carried by traders and displayed in shops as good luck talismans. Nang Kwak comes in many versions, often in the form of a small statue with a moving hand like a welcome gesture. In the version illustrated here she is a successful Tai businesswoman with long, sleek hair hanging below her waist, large bore earrings, a blouse with a decorated yoke and tubular ankle-length skirt. Good luck is reinforced by the presence of fork-tailed lizards at her side. Nang Kwak holds a pair of weighing scales and sits above a rectangular diagram of squares containing lucky letters and numbers. A border of script ensuring good luck is written around the edge of the cloth.

20. Other interpretations show the woman and horse in an embrace.

Divination Textiles

Divination is the practice of foretelling the future. In the Tai tradition it involves establishing the birth data of a client and fixing it to a specific timetable. The *saya* first asks for the day, month and year of birth. The days of the week are not counted as seven as in Western calendars but as eight. Wednesday is split into two, with one period running from midnight to before noon and the other from the afternoon to midnight. These eight time periods are paired with the planets Sun, Moon, Mars, Mercury, Jupiter, Venus, Saturn and Rahu, god of eclipses. The planets are, in turn, matched to a series of numbers described as units of cosmic power or units of life force. For those born on Sunday, they are matched to the sun and a life force of six, on Monday to the moon and fifteen, on Tuesday to Mars and a life force of eight, on Wednesday morning before noon to Mercury and a life force of seventeen, on Wednesday in the afternoon or evening until midnight to Rahu and twelve, on Thursday Jupiter and a life force of nineteen, on Friday to Venus and twenty-one, and on Saturday to Saturn and ten. Paired to the planets and life force numbers are a set of animals and the cardinal directions. Sunday is matched to a *garuda* and the cardinal direction east, Monday to a tiger and the southeast, Tuesday to a *singha* and the south, Wednesday before noon to a cat and the southwest, Wednesday afternoon to a mouse and the northeast, Thursday to a cow and the northwest, Friday to an elephant and the north, and Saturday to a *naga* and the west. The animals are not always the same and there are cultural differences. For example, the Shan depict an animal resembling a guinea pig called a *phoo* in their divination textiles. However, there are constants in divination textiles, such as the *garuda*, *naga* and *singha*, and because they are considered opposing forces the *garuda* and *naga* are placed opposite each other.

The system is more complicated when time periods are matched to lucky numbers. Those born on Saturday and Sunday in particular years in the calendar have four, six, nine and eight as their lucky numbers, while those born on Monday in specified years have seven, two and twenty. These numbers feature in personalised astrological charts. Knowing these numbers helps an individual in choosing the amount of money donated to a monastery or in selecting numbers for lottery tickets, auspicious dates for holding ceremonies and safe days to travel.

The above describes an intricate system, but in many textile paintings it is simplied. Focus is placed on particular elements, for example drawing the eight animals and adding time periods and units of life force in numbers and letters set in geometric diagrams. There are variations in the way the animals are presented such that substitutes and placements are not consistent. Three divination textiles are illustrated here for comparison. In two of them the animals are accomplished drawings, while the third is primitive. In the first sample a colourful *garuda* is represented as a prince with a lower body of feathers. In the second painting he has the head of a bird, a human torso and feathers. The third is a sketchier image with indigo the only colour used. A tiger can be clearly identified by its stripes in the first textile but is less identifiable as a tiger in the second, while in the third it ressembles a child's toy. The cow in the first textile is clearly drawn while in the second sample it is substituted by a rat, and in the third a creature that could be a cat. An elephant is represented in all three textiles, but in the first it is placed opposite a *singha*, in the second opposite a goat and in the third opposite an unidentifiable animal.

The process of establishing periods of good and bad luck begins by determining the time period the client was born, for example Tuesday with a life force of eight. Using a divination diagram like the ones illustrated here, the *saya* begins on Tuesday and moves clockwise around the chart counting up the life force in each time period until he reaches the age of the client. If the client is a woman, the movement is anticlockwise. The animal where counting stops is compared with the animal on the opposite side of the chart. For example, if the starting point is the *garuda* and the stopping point the *naga*, they are not compatible. That means the person is in a period of bad luck. The *saya* will advise the client to not undertake any important work until it passes. But as has been shown in these samples, the animals and their placement are not consistent, so a client must have faith in the calculations of the *saya* they choose to consult.

Textiles and Building

According to the *Chiang Mai Chronicle*, selecting a propitious site was the first consideration when a new Tai settlement was planned. A place was chosen where auspicious animals, like albino deer, were known to graze, because they were a sign of fertile land and a good water supply.[21] Choosing an auspicious time to begin building depended on calculations of cosmic alignment. For example, the building of the city of Chiang Mai in the thirteenth century commenced on "Thursday, the eighth waxing of the moon in the seventh month, a *kot koi* day (first day of the New Year) in the year 658, the Year of the Monkey at an auspicious early hour".[22] The alignment of the day and hour with the position of the moon, the month and the year was calculated according to a sixty-year cycle. Although not referred to in the *Chiang Mai Chronicle*, house building could also involve calculating the position of a *naga* that rotated in synchrony with a lunar calendar (see Chapter 3).

The positioning and commencement of a Tai building, whether within a city or a village, took account of the alignment of the planets, the cardinal directions, the position of the *naga* and the birth data of the person or persons for whom the building was constructed.[23] This information was recorded on cotton cloth and attached to the first house post sunk in the ground when building began. A wooden spirit house was erected in the

21. David K. Wyatt and Aroonrut Wichienkeeo, trans., *The Chiang Mai Chronicle*, Chiang Mai: Silkworm Books, 1995.

22. Sarassawadee, 2005, p. 57, and Wyatt and Aroonrut, 1995, p. 42.

23. The cardinal directions are represented in cruciform shape resembling boundary markers buried at the time of a new settlement in Chiang Rai.

grounds. On completion of the house, monks and *saya* conducted house blessing rites, recited a *paritta* and appealed to the Buddha for protection. Offerings were made to the guardian spirits at the spirit house to ensure good luck and protection. If it was a private home, the owners added their names and often stamped a handprint on the cloth. A footprint of the monk who conducted the house blessing might be added. This cloth was kept by the owner and stored in the rafters of the house. Although not intended originally for this purpose, these cloths served as proof of ownership before the era of official state registers.

Divination Cloths and the Military

Cotton cloth was used in planning military manoeuvres.[24] Outlines of the battle terrain and plans of foot soldiers and elephant and horse cavalry in formation were printed on cloth. To ensure the planets were in the correct alignment for a successful outcome, circular and square diagrams provided calculations on the periphery. The cloth was printed with incantations for protection and victory. Planning for the siege of a city meant producing maps showing defensive walls, moats and entrance gates and indicating the surrounding terrain.

Textiles printed in this way were burnt in pre-battle candle rituals. The cloth was rolled up with a cotton candle wick and inserted inside a large hollow wax candle that could be as tall as a man. It was lit at an auspicious time and incantations for victory were offered. The residual ash was collected and diluted in water for the soldiers to drink or mixed with oil and rubbed into the skin. It was believed that this ash was a recipe for victory as it magically transmitted the battle plan into the minds of the soldiers who would achieve victory. This ritual was held several days before battle commenced to give time for the magic to take hold.

24. Henry D. Ginsburg, *Thai Manuscript Painting*, London: British Museum,1989. Ginsburg describes military maps on paper in the collections of the Harvard University Arts Museum (acquisition number1984. 443).

Dress, Power and Protection

There are few printed textiles identified with the personal needs of *saya*. Generally they wear their own clothes, usually a shirt and loincloth by men and a blouse and tubular skirt in local style by women. There are exceptions, however, particularly among *saya* who are renowned for extensive tattoos that they believe make them powerful. When performing rituals they strip to a loincloth to display their extensive tattoos (see Chapter 5). *Saya* who travel carry ritual objects in bags printed with protective *yantra*. For monks, it is their robes that generate beneficial power, particularly if a monk observes many precepts as goodness which is magically absorbed into his robes.[25] Villagers come to the monastery to charge their talismans by placing them on a monk's robe. After death, a monk's robes continue to be a source of beneficial power. They are divided and distributed among the faithful. Some are used as protective backings for textile hangings and banners. Fragments become talismans, tucked in a pocket or concealed in a wallet.

Before the advent of modern battle dress, there were several ways a Tai soldier could protect himself. He could have magically charged body tattoos, wear talismanic clothing, take a drink with magically charged ash or have the ash rubbed with oil on his body. Body tattoos and talimanic clothing were printed with *yantra*, a mix of Buddhist iconography, protective spirits, comological diagrams and magic spells. Monks and *saya* were responsible for empowering them with *katha*. Talismanic vests also provided protection against injury from wild animals in the forest.

Turbans, vests, tabards, shirts and jackets were simple garments in terms of cut. Turbans were rectangular lengths of cotton. Shirts were cut from one length of cotton folded in half with a slit in the centrefold to provide a neck opening and fastened with ties at the side. Many were sleeveless although some shirts and jackets had straight-cut sleeves and front openings with

25. Before the advent of factory-produced robes, mothers or another female member of the family wove the robes, a means of gaining merit.

fastenings made from cotton cord. This was threaded with talismans, thin metal plates incised with protective script rolled up into tiny rods. The simple flat shape of these garments provided an easy surface on which to draw imagery and for writing text, generally in black ink with a few highlights added in red.

A narrow rectangular length of cotton worn as a turban could also double up as a protective armband when printed with *yantra* and empowered with magic spells and incantions. It protected against bullet wounds and magically jammed a gun pointed in the direction of the wearer. By touching the cloth and uttering the words of a magic spell, the wearer became invisible.[26] Soldiers wearing turbans and armbands of this type are illustrated in Lan Na mural paintings at Wat Buak Khrok Luang, Chiang Mai and Wat Phumin, Nan.

Talismanic tabards, shirts and jackets were probably in constant demand in the Shan and Lan Na principalities because the history of the region contains accounts of many wars and skirmishes between the two. The tribute (*muang*) system meant villagers were forcibly conscripted by their ruling prince. There was no regular army. Conscripts went to a local *saya* for a talismanic garment when they were called up. There is no record of Tai princes providing talismanic garments, but in Siam in the nineteenth century King Rama IV (1851–68) equipped his army with talismanic shirts.[27] They were probably worn when the king sent Siamese troops northwards to the Shan State of Keng Tung in 1852 and 1855.

Talismanic tabards and sleeveless shirts are printed with imagery and text on the front and back or they may have a series of *yantra* composed of squares, triangles and rectangles with Pali incantations and magic spells reduced to letters and phrases, for example a sleeveless shirt printed with twenty-five diagrams containing shorthand for the god Indra (*phya*), the

26. Information provided by the monks at Wat Tiyasathan, Chiang Mai, February 2008.
27. A private collector has a number of protective shirts issued during the reign of Rama IV.

Buddha (*ta*) and "hail to the Buddha" reduced to letters *n* and *b*. Natural forces are condensed into syllables, such as the wind *da* and the earth *ba*. *No* is *ma* repeated as a phrase to repel evil spirits. Among the figurative designs are mandala printed with the Buddha at the centre of circles of gods, humans, demons, ghosts and animals. In place of followers there are spirits depicted in aggressive mode, wielding daggers and spitting fire. Sometimes the Buddha is illustrated at the summit of a stepped diagram containing letters and numbers with protective spirits standing at the sides.

Talismanic clothing provided a shield against attack by wild animals. Nineteenth-century travellers reported on the danger and chose to sleep in trees and light large fires to keep animals at bay. The Tai recognised wild animals as having specific mental and physical attributes that were of benefit when magically transferred to them. This also applies to animal tattoos (see Chapter 6). A tiger printed on the front of a shirt, pouncing with claws extended, indicates physical power, stealth, ferocity and speed in attack. A wild pig with an accompanying *yantra* imbues the wearer with a stubborn nature and impenetrable skin to resist bullets and cuts from swords. A wild cat brings stealth and cunning and a monkey intelligence and agility.

Other illustrations seen on talismanic clothing include guardian spirits of the cardinal directions (see Chapter 2) and Phra Mae Thorani defeating the armies of the demon god Mara, a significant role model for soldiers aiming for victory. Rahu makes an appearance as a protective spirit guarding the daylight and moonlight hours. He is also presented as a frog (*poom nak kaa*) holding the full moon in his mouth, an image based on a Tai Khoen instruction to "fashion an image of Rahu the frog holding the moon in his mouth" as part of a rain-making ritual.[28] The image could also be associated with good luck. Drawings of ritual candles on the front or back of shirts suggest that candle rituals were held to protect soldiers going into battle.

---

28. Saimong Mangrai, trans., *The Paedaeng Chronicle and the Jengtung State Chronicle*, Michigan Papers on South and Southeast Asia, No. 19, Ann Arbor: University of Michigan Center for South and Southeast Asian Studies, 1981, pp. 194–95.

From the imagery illustrated on the textiles and garments in this chapter it is clear it performed an important role in explaining the workings of the universe, acting as a focus for meditation and providing forms of protection.

Cotton draw-string bags, printed with *yantra* and *katha*, property of a Shan *saya*,
(collection of Akadet Nakbunlung, Chiang Mai)

Chapter 5

CONTEMPORARY PRACTICE

Earlier chapters have focused on *yantra* and *katha* using nineteenth-century material as a source. This chapter moves to the present and explores how they are produced today and how some are reworked to suit current physical and mental health needs. Thousands of Shan have fled to Lan Na, their homes bombed or burnt by the Tatmadaw (Myanmar army). During 2024 about a thousand Shan were crossing into Lan Na each month. Many live in camps or squat illegally. As they are stateless, they no right to Thai public health facilities, and although the authorities allow some to receive treatment, many are without care. There are reports of HIV, malaria and TB as well as mental health issues brought on by anxiety, insecurity and a general feeling of helplessness. Those who find work earn low wages in jobs that citizens reject. If relatives are left behind in Shan State, they feel under pressure to send money home and are anxious about the health and well-being of their families, particularly children and the elderly.

Among the Shan who have fled across the border are monks, herbalists and *saya*. They join existing commnunities who settled and have lived in Lan Na for many years. The focus here is on monks and lay *saya* and herbalists whose work is healing, divination, creating good luck and minimising bad luck. The Shan who seek help want to know what the future holds. Will they find employment, will their families be helped and will their troubles be reduced by performing rituals and observing precepts? *Yantra* and *katha* will be part of the help they receive. In many cases it is the only help available as they are not entitled to state-funded medical care. But migrants are not the only people who consult *saya*. Well-off citizens come to augment treatments received at medical centres and they want the assurance of good luck, for example in travelling by having their motorcycles and cars blessed. But they also come for purely religious reasons, to pay respect and offer gifts to the Buddha and the spirits.

Some *saya* claim they can meditate to visualise infections caused by germs and viruses and banish the evil spirits associated with them. This is treated with disbeleief and the value of *yantra* and *katha* questioned. However, there is among doctors a recognition of the psychological benefits of ritual, especially when family and friends participate. *Saya* are also taught to identfy the symptoms of serious illnesses like HIV, TB and malaria among people who do not have the opportunity to go to a doctor. This information is passed to the relevant health authorities to follow up. Charitable bodies and non-government organisations support this approach. And *saya* and herbalists provide supplementary treatments for those who are receiving medical care. They include ointments for skin erutions, a side-effect of HIV, and cough medicine for HIV and TB sufferers.

Manuscripts continue to be a source for *saya* giving treatments. For producing *yantra,* new methods include making photocopies and scanning instead of copying by hand, and *katha* are not spoken in local dialect so often as in the past. Raw materials have changed too. Handmade mulberry paper is replaced by industrial paper and felt tip pens replace locally made ink. This is not happening everywhere and there are traditionalists using the old methods.

To report on how *saya* operate today, the author interviewed monks, lay *saya* and herbalists. They administer to Lan Na and Shan communities, to migrants and to visitors originally from the area who have moved to big cities like Bangkok and return home occasionally. The first venue is Wat Tiyasathan in Mae Daeng, Chiang Mai Province. It is situated off the main road that runs between Chiang Mai and Fang. Local residents of Shan origin helped finance the original monastery buildings and raised funds for the main Buddha image dedicated to the memory of Shan freedom fighters, the local term for soldiers in the Shan Resistance Army. In the 1960s the Thai government allowed families of insurgent leaders and their followers to settle in the area.

The abbot of Wat Tiyasathan is Phra Warinda (*paw si wan*) who was born in Shan State in 1955. He became a novice and took full vows when he was twenty, serving first in a monastery in Shan State before moving to Wat Yanara in Bangkok. From there he was sent to a monastery that he identified as Tai Yai in Paan district, Chiang Rai Province.[1] Following a request from Shan migrants working in Cambodia who wanted a Shan-speaking monk to be stationed in their area, he was sent to minister to their spiritual needs. When the dictator Pol Pot became ruler of Cambodia, Phra Warinda was sent back to Chiang Rai Province.[2] A few years later he was moved again, this time to serve at Wat Tiyasathan assisted by a community of Shan (Tai Yai) and Tai Yuan (Lan Na) monks. Phra Warinda is a member and currently Representative of the Tai Yai Buddhist *sangha*. He rarely goes to Shan State except when permission is granted for him to visit his widowed mother, his sister and her husband and their two children in Panglong. He is a modest yet charismatic man who inspires confidence among the many clients who consult him.

The congregation at Wat Tiyasathan consists of three main groups. The Tai Yuan are Lan Na people, mostly farmers, shopkeepers and businessmen. The Tai Yai are long settled having migrated to the area in the 1960s and are integrated into the community. Many are prosperous. The third group are recent arrivals, refugees and migrants from Shan State, without official documents to stay in Lan Na. They have no employment rights or health care. Phra Warinda and the monks of Wat Tiyasathan work with all these

---

1. During interviews, Phra Warinda used the term Tai Yai, not Shan, for the communities among whom he works.

2. Pol Pot ruled until 1998.

groups. They use Thai and Tai Yai language to communicate with their congregations.

When visitors come to the monastery, they pay respect to the Buddha in front of an image in the main monastery building (*vihara*). There are other buildings on site where interviews and rituals are held. The monastery has a garden with shade trees and benches so visitors can sit in pleasant surroundings while they wait for a consultation. Sometimes there are long lines of people waiting.

The simplest prescription Phra Warinda gives is a plastic bag filled with holy water blessed by monks at the monastery and used for cleansing rituals. He also distributes prayer cards and protective amulets with images of the Buddha and revered Buddhist monks that he blesses. He keeps a supply of herbal medicines and ointments in bottles and containers with labels written in Thai script. These remedies are not prepared in the monastery but obtained from herbalists and commercial companies. There are some medicinal herbs grown in small quantities in the monastery garden, but they are for the personal use of the monks.

With an extensive knowledge of Tai texts, Phra Warinda has created his own set of *yantra* and *katha*. He selects illustrations and diagrams, incantations and magic spells from Tai Yai, Tai Khoen, Burmese and Thai manuscripts that are kept in the library at Wat Tiyasathan. He emphasises that the prototypes he creates are the result of trial and error. If a particular formula is effective, he keeps it, if it does not work, he discards it or makes changes. The *yantra* are drawn on thin paper and vary in size and shape.

He describes these *yantra* in general terms as "extending life force, floating away evil from the body, mind and spirit, bringing good luck and dispensing *metta*" (Pali for loving-kindness, goodwill and harmony). The texts are written in Tai Yai and Burmese script, the latter used for writing Pali, and include letters and syllables set in codes (see Chapter 3). Phra Warinda describes the texts as *kha-tha thon-pis*, meaning "sacred words to withdraw negative power". He produces *yantra* with stylised human figures laid out individually or in pairs on each sheet of paper. They have benign facial expressions and wear stylised hats or helmets. Their hands and feet are lifelike, but their arms, legs and trunk are formed from squares, rectangles and stepped diagrams. Long and narrow *yantra* are for good luck in business. There are two sixteen-square diagrams drawn at each end of a narrow rectangular paper with borders of lucky letters and Pali incantations. These are designated spaces where Phra Warinda adds the birth data of the businessmen involved in the request. He also creates large *yantra* with two papers glued together, for example a tall *prasad* divided into squares containing letters and syllables that form stanzas from the *Metta Sutta*. A protective Pali text acts as a border. This *yantra* is used specifically in rituals for *metta*.

The set of *yantra* Phra Warinda has created are numbered. Assistant monks take them to a printing shop to make photocopies on thin transparent sheets of paper. The most popular prescriptions Phra Warinda distributes are *yantra* for burning in candle rituals. He argues that thin paper is less bulky than mulberry paper and takes up less space when rolled with a candle wick and, when required, a fragment of clothing that is inserted into the hollow wax candle. It was the sheer volume of *yantra* he needed to dispense that led Phra Warinda to develop this streamlined system with the assistance of monks and novices who ensure there is always a good supply for the abbot to prescribe.

Phra Warinda sees a steady stream of people each day as well as fulfilling the ritual and administrative obligations of an abbot. There is a mix of local people and those who have come a long distance. On a day he considered fairly quiet there were seventeen sets of visitors. Some came individually, others in groups, as well as people returning after an initial visit with supporters for a special ritual. The returnees do not necessarily see the abbot but go straight to a monastery building where a group of monks are ready to perform the ritual already prescribed.

Phra Warinda sees clients in the main *vihara* where the laity worship. He sits at a low desk and keeps manuscripts, astrological charts, books and sets of photocopied *yantra* in the drawers. Visitors sit on the floor in front of him and give an account of why they have come. Phra Warinda enquires about their personal circumstances, including the year, month and day of birth so that he can make calculations using astrological charts. This is standard for all who seek his help. Phra Warinda uses a Tai Yai calendar set according to the accession of the first Tai Yai ruler. The alternative is the Thai Buddhist Era calendar.[3] Astrological calculations are based on the Twelve-Year Animal Cycle and the Tai Yai version of the eight time period system matched to units of cosmic power (see Chapters 3 and 4). When he has gathered this information, Phra Warinda prescribes a *yantra* selected from his drawer. If the treatment includes a candle ritual, he summons a monk assistant by ringing a bell and hands the selected *yantra* to him. Phra Warinda prescribes up to three candles at a time, so the assistant will be given one to three *yantra*. He issues instructions to the assistant on the number of times the *yantra* is folded, the number of plies in the candle wick, the number of plies in the cotton yarn used to bind the wick and paper together and the number of times the binding yarn is passed around them.

A team of assistants comprising monks and novices make the ritual candles in a special area of the monastery set aside for the purpose. Laid out on a wooden table is a supply of hollow beeswax candles, a ball of beeswax, reels of cotton thread held on large spools of three, six, nine, twenty-four, thirty-eight and ninety-six plies and scissors to cut the thread. A blackboard on the wall reminds them of the number of plies and bindings for each type of *yantra* being dispensed. To assemble a candle, an assistant cuts cotton in the prescribed ply and trims it to the length of the wax candle. He folds the *yantra* into three, six or nine folds according to Phra Warinda's instructions

3. Deduct 449 years from the Buddhist Era calendar and 2553 BE becomes 2104 BE according to the Shan calendar.

and rolls the wick and paper together, binding them with cotton thread taken from the spools. Phra Warinda may instruct a fragment of the client's clothing, or a photograph, to be included. The package is inserted in a hollow wax candle. When the prescribed number of candles is ready, they are taken to Phra Warinda who chants Pali incantations and breathes over them to activate positive power. They are given to the clients with specific instructions on the auspicious time to light them and *katha* to be offered while the candles burn.

What follows is a record of one day at Wat Tiyasathan. There were busier days, but this was chosen because it provides a representative mix of divination, prescribing and counselling. The day began with a Shan refugee who walked and hitchhiked to the monastery from the Myanmar border because he had no money to pay for transport. He was unemployed and extremely anxious about his family whom he had left behind in Shan State. The abbot asked for his birth data and read his horoscope, calculating that the man was in an inauspicious phase in life. He predicted that he was in a period of bad luck that would end in two lunar months when he would find a job. The forthcoming auspicious phase of life would stay with him until he reached the age of forty-two years, when the abbot recommended that he return for another consultation. He gave the man a plastic bag of holy water for a cleansing ritual and a set of *katha* to chant for success in the future. He also gave him a small Buddha image as a protective amulet. Phra Warinda told the man he could make a donation to the monastery later when his financial situation improved.

The next client was a Shan migrant labourer worried about low wages and poor living conditions on the fruit farm where he worked. His wife and two children crossed the border with him, but they have no official papers and so he is working illegally. The abbot collected his birth data, read his horoscope and advised him he was in an auspicious phase of life that although it was hard for him and his family, no further negative forces would worsen his present condition. The abbot gave him a plastic container of holy water for a cleansing ritual and a prayer card with a picture of Phra Siwali, a disciple of the Buddha who brings good luck. The man went to pay respect to the Buddha in the main *vihara* before departing.

Phra Warinda then saw a married couple whose ancestors are Shan, but the family has lived in Thailand for three generations. The husband is a policeman and the wife a soldier in the Thai army. They had come to have their horoscopes read and to find out when they would next enter an auspicious phase that would lead to promotion. The abbot collected their birth data, consulted astrological charts and made a prediction. He gave them a blessing. They left after paying respect to the Buddha and making a donation to the monastery.

Phra Warinda then saw a young woman who came to seek advice for an eighteen-year-old friend who was too sick to travel. She had brought details of her year, day and month of birth. The abbot prescribed three candles and gave instructions to an assistant monk to fill them with three *yantra* from the series he produces. The *yantra* have human features and bodies formed from diagrams. The woman was given ritual instructions for her sick friend to follow. It included the time to light the candles and *katha* to be chanted. This was one case where the person seeking help was not physically present.

The abbot walked into the monastery grounds where two women were waiting for a ritual to protect themselves and their new motorcycles. The abbot took talismans made from cotton thread with macramé-style knots and fringes. The ply of the thread and the number of knots was set for good luck and protection. Phra Warinda attached them to the handlebars of the motorbikes, then sprinkled the women and the motorcycles with holy water while chanting incantations for good luck. The women went to the main *vihara* to pay respect to the Buddha and leave a donation.

A couple with a small child and a baby were waiting nearby in the grounds to have their new car blessed. They had brought a silver tray bearing a prayer card with an image of Phra Siwali, the monk who protects travellers and wards off misfortune. He is shown walking in a mountainous landscape.

There was also a yellow *yantra* cloth illustrated with an eight-looped diagram shaped like lotus buds and with representations of the cardinal directions protecting against evil spirits from all directions. The *katha* printed on the yellow cloth was chanted to protect the days of the week and a Pali text in shorthand describing the meritorious deeds of the Buddha (*parami*) and the Buddha's teachings (*abidhamma*). The tray also bore a small sheet of gold leaf, a pot of adhesive, sticky tape and a length of white cotton thread.

Phra Warinda asked the father to raise the hood of the car while he stood holding the silver tray. The abbot went to sit in the driver's seat of the car. He took the yellow cotton cloth from the tray and wrote a short Pali blessing on it. Using the adhesive, he attached to it the card with the image of Phra Siwali. He placed double-sided sticky tape along the back edge of the yellow cloth and pressed it in place on the windscreen and then attached the sheet of gold leaf to the windscreen above it. Throughout the process he chanted protective Pali verses. After leaving the driver's seat, Phra Warinda walked around the car spraying the engine and car body with blessed water while chanting more protective *katha*. The ritual ended and the family walked to the *vihara* to pay homage to the Buddha. They returned to sit in front of the abbot at his desk. He gave them a blessing and tied their wrists with the white cotton thread left on the offering tray. After making a donation to the monastery, the family drove away.

Two men were waiting with a request for a candle ritual to bring success in their new business partnership. Phra Warinda took their birth data, consulted an astrological chart and asked them about the type of business they were in. From his desk drawer he took two *yantra* papers with square diagrams at each end and a rectangular diagram in the middle containing letters and numbers. There were two empty squares where he wrote the names of the men and their birth data, adding the numbers two to six in a line on one side and one to seven in a line on the other. He wrote the numbers fifteen, twenty-four, thirty-six and seventy-eight and added a short Pali incantation. He rang the bell to call an assistant monk who took the *yantra* with instructions to prepare two candles. When he returned with the candles, Phra Warinda chanted *katha* and breathed on the candles before giving one to each businessman with directions on when to light them and the *katha* to be offered at that time.

The next visitor was a prosperous local lady who owns a noodle shop close to the monastery. It was her birthday, and she came with her grandson for a blessing for good luck and long life. Phra Warinda blessed her and the child. She had brought some specially cooked noodles for him and the monks and novices to eat at their pre-noon meal. She took them to the monastery kitchen and returned home.

A group of people waiting in the garden came forward to ask for a large candle for a ritual for loving-kindness (*metta*). Phra Warinda took two rectangular *yantra* that together form a *prasad* from his desk drawer. He wrote the name of the village on the papers. A monk assistant took the paper with instructions for making the large candle. He warned it would be expensive because of the amount of wax needed, charged on this occasion at one thousand and nine baht. When the assistant returned with the candle, Phra Warinda gave instructions to the group on the auspicious time to light it and on the number of ritual offerings made at the time. This involved an exact number of offering trays with a specific number of objects on each one.

The next visitor was a sick lady who came with her husband. She had been ill for some time and had already consulted a medical specialist at a local hospital and a doctor at a government clinic who had diagnosed degeneration of the bones. She claimed that although the clinic had treated her there was no improvement in her condition. Phra Warinda took her birth data and asked questions about her symptoms. He recommended a candle ritual and a *sud than* ritual to draw away evil spirits. From his desk he took three *yantra* illustrated with human figures and she handed over a small fragment of her clothing. He wrote her name and birth data on each *yantra* and summoned an assistant with instructions to make up three candles to include a fragment of her clothing in each. The candles were prepared and brought back. Phra Warinda offered incantations and breathed over them. She took them home with instructions on when to light them and the *katha* to be offered. She returned on another day for the second stage of her treatment, the *sud than* ritual, also called the *sadah kroh* ritual. She brought with her the residual ash from the burning of the three candles. A monk diluted the ash in holy water, and she took it as a drink. She sat on the floor of the *vihara* with four monks on the floor around her. They created a sacred space by passing cotton thread between them from a large spool. She held one end of the thread while a senior monk held the other end. They tied her wrists with cotton thread as a sign of binding body and spirit together. The monks chanted Pali incantations for healing and protection. Her husband sat at a distance with his hands joined in prayer. There was a final blessing before the lady and her husband left the monastery. The monks wound the cotton thread back on the spool.

A similar ceremony was held later in the day. A young sick woman came with two female and one male supporter. She sat on the floor of the *vihara* with four monks on the floor around her. They created a sacred space by passing cotton thread between them from a large spool. She held one end of the thread while a senior monk held the other end. Her friends joined her inside the sacred space formed by the cotton thread, their hands held together in prayer. A senior monk gave the sick woman a container of holy water to wash her face. Pali chanting followed, described as "withdrawing all evil". When this part of the ritual ended, the woman left the *vihara* for a few minutes and the monks rewound the cotton thread onto a spool. She returned and a monk tied her wrists with cotton thread, the left first and then the right. All four monks moved to a raised platform reserved for them at one end of the *vihara*. The woman sat in front of them on the floor with her supporters. There was chanting for healing and protection. When it ended the woman presented the monks with a tray of flowers and joss sticks. She and her supporters left for the main *vihara* to pay respect to the Buddha and make a donation before departing.

The next person to consult Phra Warinda was a young woman who was afraid evil spirits were poisoning her husband. She suspected that a polluted substance had magically entered his body, possibly rusty metal or nails, resulting in severe stomach pains. Her husband had visited a hospital clinic, but the doctors were unable to diagnose the problem. Phra Warinda took the man's birth details and diagnosed a serious condition caused by evil spirits entering his body with the polluted substance. He recommended a vegetarian diet. He took three *yantra* from the drawer in his desk, printed with *kha-tha thon-pis*, sacred words used to withdraw negative power. He called a monk assistant, instructing him to prepare three candles. When the candles were brought back, he blew on them and chanted over them. He gave instructions to the woman about the *katha* she and her husband should chant when the candles were lit. He specified the time. If the man did not recover, the abbot recommended he return to the monastery for a *sud than* ceremony. By the time this lady left it was late afternoon, and the abbot retired to his room to rest and meditate.

Wat Pang Mu

Wat Pang Mu is a monastery in Mae Hong Son, a town about twenty-five kilometres from the Shan State border. In the nineteenth century Mae Hong Son was a large village, and the capital of the region was Mok Mai. The official border between Lan Na and Shan State was drawn up in the early nineteen hundreds. Mok Mai, with predominantly Tai Yai people, was allocated to the Shan side of the border and Mae Hong Son, then mainly Tai Yuan people, to the Lan Na side. The ability to cross the border depends on the political and military situation of the time although close cultural connections continue through the Lan Na and Shan monks who are allowed to travel freely. Today the monks at Wat Pang Mu are Tai Yuan and Tai Yai. One of the Tai Yai monks taught in the Shan States before moving to Mae Hong Son ten years ago. The abbot is Tai Yuan, and he has lived at the temple for over forty years. He was born in Mae Hong Son but studied at a Shan monastery in Inlay Lake. Other monks have also spent time in monasteries in Shan State and as a result are familiar with Tai Yai *yantra* and *katha* and rituals that accompany their distribution. The community they serve today at Wat Pang Mu is a mix of Tai Yuan, Tai Yai and Tai Khoen, the latter originally from central and eastern Shan State.

Yantra prescribed at Wat Pang Mu are based on the illustrations and diagrams in manuscripts kept in the monastery library. The iconography is similar to that produced at Wat Tiyasathan although there are marked differences in the way they are copied and distributed. At Wat Pang Mu, formulae for candle rituals are copied by hand onto mulberry paper, not commercially printed paper as at Wat Tiyasathan. The monks use ballpoint pens for writing *yantra*, and the texts include Tai and Thai script. They do not prepare *yantra* to suit individuals as they come but provide pre-packaged candles with *yantra* and *katha* and instructions for use inside cellophane bags. Each bag also contains two hollow wax candles and pre-prepared cotton wicks. The bags are sealed. There are three types available. One is for good luck, the second for 'life extension', meaning good health in mind and body, and the third for *metta*.

The monks at Wat Pang Mu say they choose not to use commercial paper because mulberry paper smoulders slowly, allowing time for *katha* to be chanted properly without the words being hurried. They think commercial paper burns too quickly. Pre-packaging candles is considered acceptable because the monks claim they are familiar with the types of problems congregations have and believe most needs can be served by the three options. However, if an individual requests a special ritual, it can be arranged following an interview with a senior monk who agrees to accept the request. When questioned about the use of ballpoint pens, the monks insist it is insignificant because success depends on the power and charisma of the monk who writes the *yantra* and the power of the *katha* chanted.

Although not a regular occurrence, the monks at Wat Pang Mu perform a healing and 'long life' ritual. Offering trays are prepared for the ritual according to the number of participants. Each tray is a compilation of five stacked wooden trays decreasing in size to form the shape of a *prasad*. Each is filled with sand collected from a local riverbed and coloured paper flags (*seub chadaa*). The number of flags relates to the birth data of individual ritual participants, for example sixty-one flags if the participant is sixty-one years of age. The flags are white and red and triangular in shape. Some have floral patterns with modified *yantra* and *katha* punched into the paper. The trays are offered to the Buddha at the *vihara* while monks chant a *paritta*.

Lay *Saya*

This section examines the work of lay *saya*. Two of those interviewed have wives who are spirit mediums and the third has a mother-in-law who acts as his assistant. The first *saya* visited was Maha Kaew who lives in Pai Vieng village near Keng Tung in Shan State.[4] His prosperous-looking house is made of brick and wood and has a tiled roof. A wooden staircase on the outside of the building leads to a large room that serves as a consulting room. Textile hangings and photographs line the walls, carpets cover the floor and bottles and jars of potions and ointments are scattered around the room. Amongst a pile of modern textiles are astrological charts, lunar calendars and Buddhist banners. A portrait of His Majesty Bhumibol, the late King of Thailand, is in a prominent position on the wall.

Maha Kaew is a charismatic man who became a *saya* without any family connections to such people. At an early age he witnessed a brutal attack on his father and concluded that learning to be a *saya* would provide him with

---

4. The portrayal of women being embraced or having intercourse with animals is interpreted as a symbol of metta. Alternately, it is a symbol of magical power attained through the semen of a strong animal. It is also expressed as power from animal to animal, symbolised by a mouse suckling from a tiger.

supernatural mental and physical strength to defend himself. He decided that having his body extensively tattooed would provide supernatural protection. He underwent a long process involving thirty-two tattoo masters. His body is covered in tattoos with one layer of images over another so that his skin is almost black, except for areas around his eyes and nose, mouth and the soles of his feet. He claims this creates a magical barrier evil spirits cannot penetrate. As part of his apprenticeship, Maha Kaew learnt to copy *yantra* from mulberry paper manuscripts that belonged to a master *saya*. He also learnt *katha* by rote and how to make herbal medicines and magic potions. His rituals begin with a performance of sword dancing that he learnt from a master *saya*.

Clients who consult Maha Kaew are given a preliminary interview to establish their birth data and personal circumstances. He sets an auspicious time if there is to be a ritual and negotiates a fee. Before the ritual begins, he eats vegetarian food and wears white cotton clothes as an act of purification. The following is an account of a ritual requested for protection and good luck by a person undertaking a long journey that involved travelling on unpaved roads and crossing Burmese military checkpoints on the way to an international airport to travel overseas. These details were given to Maha Kaew during the initial interview. On the day of the ritual Maha Kaew welcomed the client and a group of supporters who sat on the floor in his consulting room. He went to change from his everyday clothes and came back wearing only a short loincloth that revealed the extent of his impressive tattoos. His mother-in-law sat in a corner of the room to act as his assistant. He began by performing a sword dance and demonstrated that his skin was impenetrable by pressing and running sharp sword blades across the surface without cutting himself. He then did the same with a large, pointed needle.

Maha Kaew sat down in front of the client and rechecked her birth data and conducted a short palm reading. He then moved around the room selecting objects from different plastic bags. He chanted and breathed over them and placed them on a tray in front of the client. These items included a white cotton cloth about the size of a small handkerchief printed with six images bordered by texts in Tai Yai script. The image in the top left of the cloth was of a woman having intercourse with a horse (see Chapter 4).[5] Next to her was a portrait of Nang Kaew, a female spirit who brings good fortune. She holds her customary weighing scales. The third image was of a naked couple embracing and the fourth image of a woman having her breasts fondled by a *garuda*. The fifth was a mouse suckling from the penis of a tiger and the sixth a woman being embraced by a *naga*. This *yantra* Maha Kaew pronounced was to generate strength, bring good luck and ensure the kindness of strangers.

Maha Kaew placed the other items he had gathered on a tray. They included the cotton *yantra* described above, two plastic jars of herbal ointment, two glass vials, one filled with white rice and plant seeds, the other containing a tiny metal cast of a couple embracing in the same stance as the *yantra* on the cloth. The glass vials had originally contained injectable medicines and had been washed and sold to Maha Kaew. One of the vials had the letters LBS LAB written on it and some Thai writing. Great importance is attached locally to injections of any kind so this vial, associated with injectable medicine, is believed to add authenticity. Maha Kaew added to one of the vials four short lengths of white and red plied cotton thread with tiny copper rods attached at the ends.[6] He added three small, sealed plastic bags containing an unidentified substance that looked like plant resin. Maha Kaew breathed on the objects and chanted over them and placed them all in one large cellophane bag. The client was told to keep the bag concealed in her clothing, and when not travelling to place it on a shelf above the level of her head. The ritual ended with a short incantation

---

5. The rods were miniature versions of those on talismanic jackets (see Chapter 4).

6. Several monks said that erroneous Pali in manuscripts of this type was common. The words were either copied incorrectly from a text or taken down incorrectly when spoken.

before Maha Kaew left the room. His mother-in-law accompanied the client and her supporters downstairs.

Kan-na and Gaysorn Rubnamtham

Kan-na Rubnamtham, also known as Sua Yen, and his wife Gaysorn live in the village of Baan Mu, a short drive from the town of Mae Hong Son. Kan-na Rubnamtham's father and previous generations of his family were *saya*. Gaysorn comes from a family of female spirit mediums. Kan-na Rubnamtham owns an old mulberry paper manuscript illustrated with *yantra* passed down through his family. It contains tattoo designs, formulae for good luck and protection, healing remedies and divination charts. The text is written in Tai Yai script with Burmese script used for writing Pali. Kan-na Rubnamtham was told by a monk that the Pali had not been written correctly. This was the response coming from several monks fluent in Pali who examined manuscripts owned by village *saya*.[7]

Unlike Maha Kaew, who has a thriving practice, the number of clients consulting Kan-na Rubnamtham has declined due, he thinks, to the location of a new hospital in nearby Mae Hong Son. It has provided villagers with access to trained medical doctors, and they now come to him only when not cured by Western medicine. For those who do consult him, he provides *yantra* copied from his manuscript onto sheets of mulberry paper. His instructions are to set the paper alight in bowls of oil while chanting *katha* that he prescribes. Kan-na Rubnamtham makes potions from the residual ash, adding herbs that are part of a secret formula. He does not make candles for rituals because he says monks in the nearby monasteries have taken over the candle ritual. He used to advise villagers on the choice of marriage partners based on birth data, and he calculated auspicious times for weddings and family events by consulting the charts in his manuscript.

---

7. A temple sleeper (khon naun tsaung) is a layperson who observes eight precepts during the Lenten retreat and meditates and attends temple ceremonies.

He is now rarely asked to do this. Nor is he asked to give auspicious times to plant and harvest rice. He claims people buy charts in the market and make their own calculations. He can no longer make a living as a *saya* so he and his wife now make thatch from dried leaves used for roofing.

Lung Ae Piya Wong

Lung Ae Piya Wong is an elderly Shan *saya*, now retired, who lives in Mae Hong Son. He was interviewed at Wat Jong Klang. He did not inherit his master's manuscript but served an apprenticeship with him for ten years. He learnt about *yantra* and divination systems, referencing them in manuscripts in the library of Wat Jong Klang. He learnt to write and chant Pali in Burmese and built a reputation among local people for skills in divination and creating powerful *yantra*. On the balcony of Wat Jong Klang, he demonstrated the way to create divination charts based on the eight-time period system. A group of monks went to the monastery library and returned with a collection of manuscripts containing Shan divination charts. Lung Ae no longer practises and is now a temple sleeper, meaning he spends his days listening to sermons and attending monastic rituals. When Lung Ae Piya Wong retired, he handed over his practice to a former apprentice, Khun Langkhu.

Khun Langkhu

Khun Langkhu is a man of about fifty who lives in Mae Hong Son. He practises in a small wooden building close to his house. It contains an array of Buddhist, Hindu and Tai statues and posters. The altar has as its main focus a small Emerald Buddha statue and a large photograph of a golden Buddha. One shelf is dedicated to the female spirits Nang Sulat Siwalee (Saraswati), Nang Thorani and Nang Kaew. Nang Sulat Siwalee appears in a colourful poster mounted on a *hamsa* bird above lotus blossoms. Nang Thorani is wringing water from her hair to cause a flood to defeat the demon god Mara. Nang Kaew is dressed in Tai style with a bag of gold in her left hand. On a lower altar shelf Khun Langkhu keeps gold and silver offering trays holding candles, fruit and flowers. Paper scrolls are arranged in front of small Buddha images. The bottom shelf has statues of local spirits and photographs of deceased members of the Shan royal family. Kept on a table to the side of the main altar is a collection of astrological charts and a variety of lengths and plies of cotton thread.

When clients come to consult Khun Langkhu they bring fruit, candles, soft drinks and joss sticks to place in front of the image of Nang Sulat Siwalee, Nang Thorani and Nang Kaew. Khun Langkhu claims particular affinity with Nang Sulat Siwalee, who is patron of education and the arts. Clients ask him to invoke her powers, particularly those studying for examinations or engaged in the performing arts. He appeals personally to Nang Sulat Siwalee for help in remembering the magic spells and incantations he uses and for performing rituals that will have the most successful outcomes. According to Khun Langkhu, the most effective days for invoking the power of Nang Sulat Siwalee are Wednesdays and Fridays in November and Saturdays and Buddhist holy days in March, calculated using astrological charts.

Sai Da and Nang Lord

Sai Da and his wife Nang Lord live in a settlement on the outskirts of Chiang Mai city with the foothills of Doi Suthep as a backdrop. Sai Da is a *saya* and Nang Lord a spirit medium. Sai Da was apprenticed to a master *saya* from Chiang Dao, a mountainous area north of Chiang Mai. Nang Lord comes from a family of female mediums and learnt the art from female relatives. Clients who consult Sai Da and Nang Lord are primarily Shan people living on the Thai side of the border. Sai Da and Nang Lord have a small house in which the living room is used for their practice. A small courtyard at the front provides a shady place where clients can sit and wait to be seen. In the main living room are cupboards filled with ritual paraphernalia and gifts from clients. Posters of the Buddha and revered monks line the walls.

To begin the day, Sai Da pays respect before a photograph of his master from Chiang Dao. When patients arrive to consult him, he prescribes *yantra* for good luck, protection and loving-kindness (*metta*). He does not keep *yantra* readily available for all treatments. There are clients who arc asked to return to collect special *yantra* they have requested as he has to produce these from scratch. Because of a lack of space in the living room, he prepares *yantra* while seated at a low collapsible table. He uses mulberry paper that he buys in a local market and ballpoint pens, graphite pencils and a ruler to draw *prasad*. Some clients consult Sai Da and Nang Lord following treatment at government clinics because they want to make sure they have the best chance of a cure.

At the time of the visit, Sai Da was in the process of drawing a *yantra* on a large sheet of mulberry paper. He had already drawn three diagrams in the shape of boundary stones (*sima*) and was now drawing the fourth. This *yantra* will include a *prasad* and takes a whole day to complete, with diagrams filled with letters and symbols to represent stanzas from the *Metta Sutta*. It has been commissioned by a Shan group who worship at a local monastery and is to be inserted in a large hollow wax candle as part of a ritual for *metta*.

Sai Da prepares smaller *yantra* on sheets of mulberry paper that Nang Lord keeps in a sealed tin. She says Sai Da is familiar with the difficulties clients face and prepares *yantra* to deal with the most common problems. Nang Lord produces from the tin a small lifelike pencil drawing on mulberry paper of a water buffalo with letters and symbols written inside the body and around the border. This, Sai Da explained, was a *yantra* to drive away evil spirits because evil spirits are afraid of water buffalo. He says it is a popular *yantra* among clients and he produces several copies at a time cut from one large sheet of mulberry paper. Also in the tin is a *yantra* he prescribes when married couples are not getting along well. It depicts a man and woman with their heads at each end of the mulberry paper, their arms extended and their legs apart, with the soles of the feet touching each other. The letter 'k' is written on their chests with letters and symbols for harmony. He produces another *yantra* for healing and protection which is composed of diagrams containing letters and phrases with enclosed loops representing protective enclosures that evil forces cannot penetrate. Guardian spirits are drawn in the corners of the inner squares of the *yantra* to defend against evil spirits. Sai Da gives instructions to his clients when he prescribes these papers. Most are for candle rituals or for burning in bowls of oil. He makes hollow candles from beeswax he buys in a local market, and issues candles singly or in sets of two or three. He adds the name and birth data of clients to the *yantra* at the time they are prescribed. If a healing ritual is involved, he asks for a fragment of clothing to add with the paper. Without personal markers he says beneficial spirits are not able to recognise the client.

Nang Lord practises in the same room as Sai Da. When calling the spirits, she changes into a special ankle-length Tai skirt and blouse kept to hand. Nang Lord also runs a successful herbal medicine practice. Basic ingredients are wild honey and herbs that she collects on auspicious days, calculated according to a lunar calendar. She says the days are limited to four or five each year. Before she begins making potions, she offers the honey and herbs to the spirits for a blessing. She grinds and blends the ingredients, producing up to ten different types of ointment. Nang Lord does not divulge the secrets of her recipes to outsiders but admits to selecting plants that have auspicious-sounding names as well as for their healing properties. She uses small plastic pots as containers and keeps them in one of the storage cupboards. Clients come to her mainly to treat headaches and sleeplessness, burns and skin rashes. She also distils herbs into small soap-like cakes. One contains *sompoy* (*Acacia rugata*), used in cleansing rituals and prescribed diluted in water as a soothing wash for babies and small children who cry a lot.

Nang Lord and Sai Da cooperate in their work. They have one young man who comes for treatment of the symptoms of HIV infection. Sai Da prepares *yantra* for healing rituals and Nang Lord treats his physical symptoms.

She gives him ointment for skin eruptions and herbal medicines for a cough and diarrhoea, both symptoms of HIV. Their treatment is supplementary to the treatment he receives at a local hospital where doctors give free samples donated by a drug company. In exchange he takes part in clinical trials.

In conclusion, the *yantra* and *katha* produced today can be traced to records in mulberry paper manuscripts. They have been adapted to suit the needs of today. *Saya* streamline the process of creating *yantra* using modern technology, particularly in areas where large numbers of people seek help from charismatic *saya* who do not have time to handwrite *yantra* for each client. They rely on assistants to help. This is by no means the norm. *Saya* with small, thriving practices handwrite *yantra* on mulberry paper and keep a stock of supplies. However, many *saya* have seen their practices shrink as government medical services improve and people calculate horoscopes themselves using books from the market or go online and search the Internet for consultations.

When life in Lan Na and the Shan States revolved around the annual cycle of rice production, women made ritual offering trays during quiet periods in the cycle when their labour was not needed in the fields. Today there is no break in production as multiple cropping systems and modern irrigation schemes mean crops are grown almost continuously. Many women have left farming completely and now work in regular employment in factories and offices and in the thriving tourist industry. Ritual materials are now factory-made. There is some opposition to this from traditionalists who believe in the power of natural, handmade materials. Spirits come, they say, when attracted by the perfume of pure beeswax candles and *yantra* on mulberry paper. In terms of treating disease, they argue, *saya* are effective because they produce healing *yantra* and ritual chanting calms the mind and body. At the time of death, it eases their passing.

CHAPTER 6

TATTOOS

Tattooing the body is an ancient tradition in Southeast Asia. The Chinese who produced the first written records reported that the people on their southern borders wore 'skin garments', interpreted as meaning they were tattooed. Chinese records of the fourth century CE refer specifically to tattooed P'u people.[1] The Tai adopted the custom, and extensive tattooing on specific areas of the body was common practice among the Tai of Lan Na and Shan State.[2] The purpose of tattoos was not merely to decorate the body, although that was important, but also a way to gain power. Men with a set of body tattoos and the correct *katha* and Buddhist incantations to activate them, were confident that humans and spirits would treat them with respect.[3] Writing in the nineteenth century, the British administrator Sir George Scott noted that Shan tattooists had a great reputation: "Mostly all the men who tattoo charms and cabalistic figures are Shans. They claim and are allowed a special skill in such matters, and as they mutter spells and incomprehensible incantations over the 'medicine' are looked up to with profound belief and a very considerable awe."[4]

1. D. G. E. Hall *A history of South-East Asia,* London, Macmillan, 1955, p. 153

2. Carl Bock, *Temples and Elephants: Travels in Siam in 1881–1882,* 1884, reprint Singapore: Oxford University Press, 1986, pp. 170–74.

3. Nicola Tannenbaum,'Tattoos: Invulnerability amnd Power in Shan Cosmology', *American Ethnologist,* 1987, 14 (4) :696–97

4. Sir J. George Scott, *Burma: A Handbook of Practical Information,* 1906: reprint Bangkok: Orchid Press 1999.

Tattoos were created to ward off evil spirits and protect the body against sickness and injury. As Sir George noted, they were referred to as 'medicine' although they had powers beyond that. Specific tattoos have the power to create popularity and bring success in love, others to gain respect and be treated with generosity in the community and among strangers. Certain tattoos can be activated to make a person invisible by touching the image while offering invocations to a legendary tattoo master. These tattoos are a force for good, but some tattoos meant for good purpose can spiral out of control to cause harm. Among them is the tiger tattoo that in the past was intended as a defensive mechanism for active soldiers and those working in the forests where they were likely to be confronted by dangerous wild animals.[5] Young men can have themselves tattooed with tigers for different reasons, magically transferring the power and brute force of the tiger to create violent and aggressive behaviour individually or in gangs. Warnings written in the manuscripts make it clear that the tiger tattoo was always a dangerous image to work with, and other tattoos are listed for possible misuse. Learning about the mishandling of tattoo images is included in training apprentices.

Apprentices come from families who for generations have been tattooists although there are some men without connections who seek a master willing to take them on. An apprenticeship involves more than the practicalities of handling and sharpening the needles and mixing the ink. One must learn the art of meditation, the special rituals associated with tattooing, the meaning and use of individual tattoo images and the *katha* that activate them. Because many apprentices had already served the customary three-month period as novice monks, they had acquired a basic knowledge of Pali phrases that could be used with *katha* to empower tattoos. A tattoo apprenticeship seems to have gone on for a long period, some informants

---

5. Today tigers are on the brink of extinction. A modern temple in the hills near Keng Tung is dedicated in their memory.

say up to ten years. If his master retired or passed away, he inherited the tattooing equipment and manuscripts. This was an important legacy as ownership of a tattoo manuscript and equipment passed down through a lineage of tattoo masters brought power to the new owner. Its placement on a special altar with other ritual materials and its purification with holy water at New Year indicates the value and respect afforded to it. This equipment was carried in a special box or a cotton bag printed with protective *yantra* when the tattooist travelled to see clients.[6]

When he is judged skilled enough to be a tattoo master, an apprentice goes through an induction ceremony. He fasts, wears white clothing and drinks ash from burnt mulberry paper tattoo illustrations, diluted in water. Some records claim that men drank the ash of tattoo manuscripts as part of induction rituals, but as such manuscripts were passed down from one generation to the next it seems unlikely this was a regular custom. Before a tattooing session begins, a propitious day is chosen through calculations of the power of the moon and the birth data of the individual being tattooed. The night of a full moon in November is considered the most auspicious. The candidate prepares himself by cleansing his body and spirit of impurities. He observes the Five Precepts of no killing of a living being, no stealing, no falsehoods, no adultery and no consumption of alcohol. There may be dietary restrictions and other restraints. These include avoiding walking under washing lines that have women's lower garments hanging from them and abstaining from sexual relations. It is believed that men are weakened by contact with menstrual blood and vaginal secretions.[7] The candidate must also refrain from showering during the week before he is tattooed.

Tattooing sessions are often held on a raised wooden platform or beneath a cloth canopy, or in a special room set aside for the purpose. There is

6. San San May, 'Tattoo Art in Burmese Culture', Southeast Asia Library Group Newsletter 43, London December 2011, p. 8

7. B.J. Terweil, *Monks and Magic: An Analysis of Religious Ceremonies in Central Thailand*, 1994, 3rd reprint, Bangkok: White Lotus, 2001, pp. 78–79

a special altar dedicated to the spirits where, on the appointed day, the candidate places offerings of flowers, incense sticks and a beeswax candle. He pays a fee that has already been agreed, the amount set to include the number six or multiples of six, an auspicious number. The candidate kneels in front of the altar that faces east, lights the beeswax candle and incense sticks and makes obeisance to an ancestor tattoo master. For his part, the tattooist ensures the area is secluded and peaceful. There must be no menstruating women or pregnant women or the husbands of pregnant women in the vicinity.[8]

On completion, a newly tattooed man is expected to continue to keep at least one of the Five Precepts observed during the preparatory stage. The exception is when extremely powerful tattoos are created. Then the candidate must swear an oath to continue observing the Five Precepts and refrain from eating offal, certain named vegetables and meals served at funerals. If a candidate fails to keep the Five Precepts, there are negative consequences of illness and, at worst, insanity. Failure to observe food restrictions leads to a painful illness.

Being tattooed gave men a standing in society, a relative judgement that depended on the extent of the tattoos and the pain endured during the process. If a man had large areas of his body tattooed, for example from waist to knee or waist to ankle, it was a symbol of courage and endurance and a mark of the passage from youth to manhood. Young men with extensive tattoos became suitable candidates for marriage. Tattoos had an equally important aesthetic value, sexually attractive to women who delighted in their appearance. The process was described as "being made beautiful forever". [9] Until the middle of the last century, young women expected an eligible male to have a set of tattoos from waist to knee. Not all men conformed and those without tattoos were labelled 'unripe' or 'not cooked'.

8. Interview with Kan-na Rubnamtham, Mae Hong Son, January 2010.

9. Susan Conway, *Thai Textiles,* London, British Museum Press, 1992, pp. 112–13

Tattooing as a rite of passage can be compared with entering a monastery as a novice monk. Both are markers of transition from youth to manhood.

The Tattooing Process

Outlines of tattoos are drawn freehand on the surface of the skin. A wooden stamp is used for popular designs. Some experienced tattooists skip the drawing process and go straight to tattooing. The tattoo needle has a heavy handle that acts as a weight to steady the hand. Three sharp hand-forged blades with longitudinal grooves hold the ink. Serrated plates in different sizes and patterns have sharp points for tattooing border patterns. The ink is black, red or colourless. Black ink, the most common, is made from burnt animal fat, soot from a kitchen fire and bile from a pig, bear or bull.[10] These ingredients guarantee the tattoos will not fade. Red ink is made from cinnabar (mercury sulphide) mixed with animal bile and is generally restricted to isolated tattoos on the upper body. The disadvantage is that red ink is prone to fading, and working with it also requires a level of caution. A tattoo master claimed that a tattooer could go mad if he drank alcohol while tattooing with red ink. Ingredients added to tattooing ink include ground herbs, shavings from powerful objects and, according to Sir George Scott, house lizard skins. The house lizard is an auspicious animal (see Chapter 4). Another auspicious ingredient is the exfoliated skin of a monk.[11] The third type of ink, made from sesame or coconut oil, is invisible on the surface of the skin but considered just as powerful as visible tattoos when activated with appropriate *katha*. Tattoos are redrawn if the ink fades and need to be re-empowered from time to time as they do not maintain power indefinitely. A man will return to a tattooist for the re-empowering ritual.

10. Bock, *Temples and Elephants*, p. 17

11. Leslie Milne and Wilbur Willis Cochrane, *Shans at Home*, 1910, reprint Cornell University Library, 2009.

The speed at which tattooists worked varies. Sir George Scott wrote that the tattoo artist who worked on him was experienced and produced fifteen figures in a little over half an hour.[12] He describes youths who boasted of having a complete set of leg tattoos in one session although Scott thought this was unlikely. Elderly men with traditional tattoos from waist to knee said the process took two days, one day for each leg. They informed Scott that a man who wanted to continue and have his back, chest and arms tattooed waited a few days to recover from the pain of the first two sessions although opium was available for pain relief.

Scott encountered many men who were tattooed from waist to knee or waist to ankle with tattoos on their chests and backs. There were local names, for example tattoos from waist to ankle were known as *shan baung-bi*. Scott described them as 'old style' tattoos that he said prevailed in 'jungle districts'. This implies different forms of tattooing in rural areas and towns as well as class difference. This was not the perception of other travellers who wrote that *shan baung-bi* tattoos were common among all classes, including the princes of Lan Na and the Shan States. The German explorer Carl Bock wrote that the Tai courts retained their own tattoo artists. In the 1880s when he visited the court of the prince of Muong Li, Bock wrote: "At last he [the Prince of Muong Li] presented himself in great pomp, dressed in striped yellow and black silk … a large white calico dressing gown reaching below his knees, half hiding his thin calves which were tattooed all over."[13]

To have extensive tattoos from waist to knee was the custom among Tai soldiers, as portrayed in nineteenth-century mural paintings. The soldiers are depicted riding elephants and on horseback, with loincloths tucked high on their thighs to reveal the extent of their tattoos.[14]

12. Shway Yoe (Sir James George Scott), *The Burman: His life and Notions,* Vol I, 1882, London, Macmillan; reprint New York: W.W. Norton, 1963, p. 41.

13. Bock, *Temples and Elephants*, pp. 170–74

14. For example, Wat Buak Khrok Luang, Chiang Mai and Wat Phumin.

Tattooing had side-effects, probably due to a lack of hygiene. The skin swelled and caused irritation, made worse by scratching that led to skin lesions that could quickly become infected. Tattooists prescribed herbal remedies to alleviate the symptoms. Some men could not face the pain involved in undergoing a complete set of tattoos having witnessed the unpleasant side-effects suffered by others. They opted for a few tattoos for protection. In the past, small balls of mercury, iron and orpiment were inserted through incisions in the skin, and for those who could afford it rubies, fine gold wire and gold and silver discs printed with *yantra*. These inserts created hard, raised areas under the skin that were overlaid with tattoos. Both procedures were carried out by tattooists. In the nineteenth century, the British surveyor Holt Hallett observed: "It is not at all uncommon to meet a Shan with several knobs on his chest, concealing the talismans that he has inserted as charms to render him proof against bullet and sword." This practice is now rare and only a few elderly men bear the tell-tale signs of hard, raised skin.[15]

Tattoo Manuscripts

Tattoo manuscripts contain designs, texts and instructions on the necessary rituals. Clients can select the designs they want and choose where they are placed on the body. Sir George Scott, writing at the time under the pseudonym Shway Yoe, described them as 'sample books': "The best *saya* carry about sample books with them containing clever drawings from which the aspirant may select the patterns he likes best and mark their relative positions before he takes the opium."[16]

In Lan Na and the Shan States, tattoo script is written in *kham meuang*, Dua Tham, Tai Yai, Burmese or Khmer script. Some tattoo masters consider

---

15. Holt S Hallet, *A thousand Miles on an Elephant in the Shan States,* London: William Blackwood and Sons 1890, reprint Bangkok, White Lotus, 1988, p. 138

16. Shway Yoe, *The Burman,* p. 42

Khmer script to be the most powerful. Dua Tham and Burmese script are used for writing Pali incantations, often in shorthand unless they run along the whole area of the body in which case they can be complete texts. *Yantra* diagrams containing astrological calculations, birth data and magic words are present in encrypted diagrams (see Chapter 3). Some designs require special preparations. Tattooed images of the Buddha are one example.

The five-Buddha image of Krakucchanda, Kanakamuni, Kacyapa, Gautama and Maitreya requires the recipient to observe the Five Precepts and dietary restrictions and prepare a special platform or canopy where the tattooing will take place. Buddha images are tattooed in a process that involves chanting Pali incantations while the tattoo needle makes the pricks to the skin. This is a powerful tattoo, and when completed the recipient swears to observe the Five Precepts for all time. A Buddha tattoo provides a general shield against evil spirits and can, with additional incantations, be activated for protection against bullet wounds and cuts from knives and swords.[17]

Tattoos of gods and goddesses from the Buddhist pantheon were chosen for specific attributes. Students, academics and public figures favoured a tattoo of the goddess Saraswati who improved reading skills and levels of concentration for study. The goddess Nang Thorani helped the recipient speak clearly and be easily understood. Tattoos of brahmins brought intelligence and the ability to retain information with a good memory. As a legendary scholar, the brahmin Gavampati was a popular image and the brahmin Bharivisati brought all-round academic achievement.

Tattoos of animals were popular, as Carl Bock noted. The Tai he encountered were mostly tattooed from waist to knee with life-like animals and birds and what he termed 'emblematic monsters'. A master tattooist provided Bock with a list of the most popular animals for leg tattoos. They were rats, pigeons, vultures, lions, bats, civet cats, tigers, elephants, monkeys,

17. Information provided by Kham Indra, Chiang Mai 2009.

rachasee (king of beasts) and Hanuman, lord of the monkeys.[18] Animal attributes could be transferred by stroking the tattoo image while chanting a spell.

The *rachasee* is the symbol associated with power and protection. The elephant as an auspicious animal was the harbinger of good luck. A civet cat brought the attributes of dexterity, speed and stealth, and some men said a civet cat tattoo on the lower arm protected against insect bites. Having tattoos of both a tiger and a civet cat was considered particularly effective. A monkey tattoo brought the physical attribute of agility, intelligence and alertness and the monkey is a symbol for longevity. A sacred goose (*hamsa*) brought success in business and travel. *Kinnara* and *kinnari*, half-human, half-bird, are tattooed in pairs. They have artistic attributes, and their tattoos are favoured by singers, actors, musicians and those who speak in public, such as politicians. A tattoo of a wild pig gave a fearless nature and a thick, resilient skin. It enabled the human body to withstand bullets, sword and knife cuts, beatings with sticks and the bites and sharp tearing claws of wild animals. A tattoo of a house lizard with a forked tail brought good luck and the loving kindness of strangers, its unique call transcribed in tattoos as a phonic spell. It is a popular image among traders and shopkeepers.

Although the *naga* occurs in *yantra*, it is not popular as a tattoo image because of its association with branding prisoners.[19] A tattooist told Bock that tiger tattoos were for soldiers and workers whose occupations involved physical danger. Scott encountered many Shan soldiers and bandits on his travels who, he noted, had tigers tattooed on their chests and upper arms. Men chose tigers because they believed the natural instincts and physical characteristics of a tiger could be magically transferred to them. The tiger image was adopted by American soldiers during the Vietnam War as the

18. Bock, *Temples and Elephants,* pp. 170–74.

19. Tom Vater and Aroon Thaewchtturat, *Sacred Skin* Visionary World Ltd., Bangkok 2011, p. 61

legend of the tiger captured imaginations. Elderly tattooists remembered American soldiers among their clients in the 1970s.[20] The tiger tattoo generally portrays the animal with a snarling countenance in the action of pouncing with claws extended. It is similar to images drawn on talismanic shirts (see Chapter 4). Today construction workers often choose a wild pig tattoo as a form of protection against accidents that are common on poorly supervised building sites.

Extensive body tattooing was a male custom. Tai women were only tattooed with small dots in isolated areas of the body or on the face. Three dots forming a triangle were tattooed on the forehead or the chin. Dots tattooed on the tongue were in the shape of the letter 'o', shorthand for *om mani padme hum*.[21] These tattoos were believed to provide protection against illness, while dots on the hands and legs, particularly near the ankles, protected against insect bites.

Although tattoo images are generally intended for positive use, they can be a negative force. Civet cat tattoos, associated with dexterity, speed, and stealth, are attributes useful to criminals when evading capture and can turn the recipient into a grotesque superman capable of outstanding feats of athleticism, performing criminal acts with the ferocity of an evil spirit. The fearless nature of a wild pig with its thick, resilient skin is a tattoo popular with street gangs needing protection against weapons wielded by rival gangs. Thugs with tiger tattoos used tiger attributes to disrupt and terrify local communities. A tattoo of the ogre spirit *phi lo* is invoked to exorcise evil spirits that possess humans, but this can be reversed when a gruesome ritual is performed to turn *phi lo* into a negative force. Sir James Scott describes how a man was forced to eat the flesh of a corpse while undergoing the reverse process, while another was compelled to gnaw on human bones.[22]

20. An elderly monk at Wat Pang Mu, Mae Hong Son tattooed US soldiers fighting in Vietnam.

21. Shway Yoe, *The Burman*, pp. 41–47.

22. Shway Yoe, *The Burman: His Life and Notions check page number*

Whether Scott witnessed the actual ritual or was reporting it second hand is not clear.

Scott also describes how a man was tattooed with an image of the evil spirit Bawdithada and took on his attributes by wandering among graves looking for human bones to chew.[23] The man became a lunatic with an aggressive, restless and unpredictable nature, feared in the community as a potential murderer. Reversing this terrible downward spiral required the intervention of revered monks who observed many precepts. Scott noted that if their ministrations were not successful, an assassin was hired to kill the man while he was sleeping When a client insisted on having a tattoo image that could be manipulated for evil purposes, the tattooist used subtle ways to reduce its power if he suspected the intentions of his client. Unknown to the recipient he could omit a vital detail from the tattoo or leave out words from the *katha* that empowered it. Or he could encircle the image with a Pali incantation. But danger did not just come from the actual tattoo image. It could be from the words of a *katha* that negatively charged it.

During the research for this book, the author visited elderly monks with extensive tattoos living in a cave at the Pa Daeng shrine near Mae Hong Son. They had withdrawn from their monastery. One of the monks was born in Shan State but had moved to Thailand with his family during childhood. He had extensive tattoos on his chest, back and arms and *shan baung-bi* tattoos from waist to ankle. The tattoos on his chest and arms were overlaid with Pali texts, making it difficult to distinguish images from writing. The overall impression was of a long-sleeved black vest. Tattooing one layer over another, he argued, creates a magic barrier that evil spirits cannot penetrate.[24] The second monk living in the cave was extensively tattooed on the chest with square *yantra* diagrams containing Shan and Burmese letters

23. Bawdithada was a king who became a cannibal. He was eventually saved by the power of the Buddha.

24. Another example in this book is *saya* Maha Kaew from Keng Tung who was tattooed by thirty-two tattoo masters (see Chapter 5).

that gave the overall impression of a breastplate. He had tattoos on his upper arms of *yantra* and Pali texts that extended as far as his wrists. His back was tattooed with civet cats, a wild pig and a cow and a set of square and circular *yantra* that he claimed provided overall protection.

The author interviewed Shan tattooists and clients to establish current working conditions. They are men who have either lived in Lan Na since childhood or continue to live in Shan State but come across the border to hold tattooing sessions in cities and villages in Lan Na. They attract clients locally as well as some who travel long distances to be tattooed by a particular master. This is a legacy from a time before the border with Myanmar closed when well-known Shan tattooists crossed legally to hold tattooing sessions. Today some are prepared to cross illegally if there are enough clients. One who was waiting was a 39-year-old man living near Wat Huaipha, close to Mae Hong Son town. In preparation for the imminent arrival of the tattooist he is keeping the Five Precepts, observing food taboos and abstaining from contact with women. He has chosen a set of *yantra* tattoos he describes as 'charm diagrams' that he will have tattooed on his back, and for each arm nine-square *yantra* diagrams and protective texts. He has chosen these tattoos for three reasons: to make him popular wherever he goes, for power to attract the opposite sex and to protect himself against all forms of injury.

His older colleague, Khun Yai, from the same village, was tattooed over thirty years ago by a tattooist who came over the border from Shan State. He said it cost 250 Thai baht, which was expensive at the time. He had a five-Buddha image tattooed on his upper back. In preparation for this tattoo, he had been told to construct a special platform. He was tattooed on the lower back with an image of a wild pig encircled with protective text, and on his inner thigh a bird tattoo, a rendition of a *kinnara*. He chose the five-Buddha image and the wild pig for overall physical and mental protection and the *kinnara* to enable him to speak clearly and persuasively. At the time he was tattooed thirty years ago, some men were still choosing to be tattooed from waist to knee and knee to ankle. He said he was not prepared to face the pain of such extensive tattoos and claimed there were many other men like him. There was less pressure to conform to earlier customs that looked on tattoos from waist to ankle as a symbol of maturity and attractiveness to women. Khun Yai argued that women could be equally charmed by carefully selected tattoos.

The author also visited a monk at Wat Pang Mu in Mae Hong Son who was a lay tattooist before taking orders in middle age. Wat Pang Mu is one of the oldest temples in the district with a *chedi*, a Buddhist stupa, dated to the fifteenth century. It is there, with permission from senior monks that he practises on condition that tattoos are only for positive power. Being fluent in Pali language and texts and keeping Buddhist precepts makes him a particularly powerful tattooist although he had a large following before being ordained. He tattoos local men and those who cross from Shan State. He also has Thai clients coming mainly from Bangkok and other big cities. During the Vietnam War in the 1970s, his clients included American soldiers.

In Chapter 1 the nature of *saiyasart*, a term for 'not strictly Buddhist' or 'dealing with worldly issues', was raised. The way tattooing is treated at Wat Pang Mu indicates a similar approach taken at a practical level. The room where the monk tattoos clients is located away from the main monastery buildings at the back of the compound. It thus creates a physical distance between what is considered *saiyasart* and the buildings where Buddhist rituals are held. The altar appears to be a temporary fixture, assembled from three folding tables, perhaps meant to be easily dismantled if the liberal attitude of senior monks towards *saiyasart* should change. Laid out on the altar are donations, including an enamel bowl containing a set of monk's robes wrapped in cellophane, fresh fruit and flowers, paper flags and incense sticks. Before the monk begins tattooing, candles and incense sticks are lit and prayers offered to an ancestral tattoo master.

The tattoo needles the monk uses were inherited from a family member while he was working as a lay tattooist. They had passed down through four generations of his family. He has two sets of needles with brass angels (*thep*) carved on the heavy metal handles. He shares his recipe for tattoo ink that involves burning a candle on the back of a plate, scraping off the ash and mixing it with the gall bladder of a fish or monkey before adding fine shavings from a local red stone that he claims has great power, an ingredient that is one of many esoteric components added to tattoo ink.

The monk no longer owns the family tattoo manuscript because it was sold. He did not say why, but it is likely it was bought by a dealer. Tattoo manuscripts with their unusual spirit illustrations are popular among dealers who regularly tour villages for antiques. They separate the folios and sell the illustrations individually as framed pictures, fashionable among interior decorators and tourists. Before the manuscript was sold, the monk copied the designs and texts in a notebook with a ballpoint pen. He has copied *yantra* with illustrations of animals, spirits and geometric diagrams. Attached to the front cover of the notebook is an astrological chart written in central Thai script that he uses for calculating auspicious times for tattooing.

In a village near Mae Hong Son lives the elderly tattooist Kan-na Rubnamtham. He and his wife migrated to Mae Hong Son from Shan State over four decades ago to set up a new practice. He was apprenticed to a family member in Shan State who was a tattooist and a *saya* who distributed mulberry paper *yantra* for healing and protection. Like his father, Kan-na Rubnamtham operated a general practice until recently when age forced him to slow down. He was a well-known *saya* with clients in Mae Hong Son town and villages nearby and was prepared to travel further when asked. Kan-na Rubnamtham owns a mulberry paper manuscript which he inherited from his father.[25] The tattooing designs are animals, angels (*thep*) and *yantra* diagrams for healing and protection. There are also astrological charts. Kan-na Rubnamtham is tattooed on his chest, arms and thighs with animal and human spirits, Buddhist icons and *katha* texts.

25. It passed down to his father from a *saya* ancestor called Maha Jing.

Kan-na Rubnamtham is frail and concerned that no one in the family is interested in taking over his practice. He worries about the legacy of tattooing and cultural values that may be lost. He views tattoos and tattoo manuscripts as expressions of ethnic and cultural identity and argues they should be considered for conservation by local religious authorities. This would go some way towards halting their loss and preventing them from being degraded to the level of interior design. He wants to keep his tattoo manuscript in the family in the hope that it can be passed to someone willing to continue his practice. If that does not happen, the manuscript will be donated to a local monastery where he hopes the monks will care for it. If they accept the manuscript, it will undergo a purification ritual before being placed in the monastery library. Kan-na Rubnamtham remains determined the manuscript is not sold to a dealer. He believes the younger generation are not interested in old tattoo designs and texts and do not respect power passed down from ancient masters.

It is true that the young prefer fashionable tattoo parlours in the major cities like Bangkok. Kan-na Rubnamtham is out of step with the times, as he believes modern tattoos are meaningless and culturally damaging. It is true that in major urban centres tattooists draw on local sources, but there are the same characters, gods, goddesses and spirits although they are dressed in the style of Thai puppets and *Ramayana* dancers. The fears Kan-na Rubnamtham expresses are genuine as young men leave the rural areas for better paid jobs in cities and choose to be tattooed away from their villages. Tattoos are now part of fashion set by pop and movie stars, footballers, characters in Thai soaps and horror movies who feature on websites and city billboards. Stars like Angelina Jolie, who has a high profile in Southeast Asia, have helped popularise tattoos among women.[26]

Although the tattoo debate continues, there are some practices that have not disappeared. Young men still become apprentices but not to just one

26. Acharn Noo Kampai tattooed Angelina Jolie in 2003 and 2004.

master. For example, in Bangkok they follow several, called *acharn sak* or *sak yant*, and put together their own repertoires of tattoo images, *yantra* and *katha*, some old, some new. They continue to learn Pali incantations and letters in the Khmer alphabet for writing powerful spells. Like the tattooists in Lan Na and Shan State, *acharn sak* can be practising monks or laymen. The most popular *acharn sak* in Bangkok welcome a steady stream of clients to their tattooing shrines. A popular *acharn sak* works quickly to deal with the large numbers waiting for his services.

Many clients choose *acharn sak* according to the famous people they have tattooed. Some become international celebrities and travel abroad to other Asian countries like Singapore where they have many followers. As in the past, they are physically impressive, with extensive body tattoos (see Chapter 5). They wear amulets as a link to hermits (*ruesi*) who they claim are the original tattoo artists and *ruesi* masks while tattooing their clients. They have colourful shrine rooms with altars bearing images of the Buddha along with statues of Chinese and Hindu gods and goddesses. Clients bring flowers, incense, candles and other gifts to place on the altar, as is the tradition.

Preparation for tattooing can be the same as in Lan Na and Shan State. The client observes the Five Precepts and accepts dietary and sexual restrictions. As there are now women clients, they are expected to observe the same rules. Taboos associated with monks and their relationship to women prevents them from tattooing women. However, more and more women are choosing to have tattoos when they work on construction sites and are employed in other hazardous occupations such as road building. A woman told the author her tattoos had protected her from being shot during a recent government demonstration in Bangkok.

In terms of modern equipment, tattooing needles are made of stainless steel, and some *acharn sak* use electric tattoo machines although they are not universally popular. Designs are first marked on the skin with a pen or a tattoo stamp. Tattoo ink is bought commercially, and as with recipes from earlier times is mixed with animal bile and ingredients like herbs and house lizard skins. Incantations and spells are chanted over the ingredients as they are prepared. Invisible tattoos are produced using sesame oil and herbs. Tattoo needles are sterilised as most *sak yant* are aware of the dangers of infection from contaminated needles. Some choose to wear rubber gloves to protect themselves.

In conclusion, Bangkok has many famous media personalities who influence young men and women on the type of tattoos they choose. Meanwhile, tattooists in rural areas continue to lose customers while criticising trends away from 'traditional' tattooing. In a wider context, this is an argument about authenticity and rural Tai culture in comparison with modern city values. It is also about tattoos and power, respect for tattoo ancestors and fear that tattoos will be reduced to just a form of decoration. There is strength in the argument that tattooing will become standardised and lose its ethnic and regional identity. In practical terms, this means a loss of indigenous script and local designs and the forfeiting of local language and dialects. It is impossible to halt change, but it is possible to ensure that tattoo manuscripts from Lan Na and the Shan States are conserved as important records of the past. They should be stored in museums and monastery libraries where they can be accessed for research and education.

A tattoo needle with a brass handle decorated with an angel (*thep, thewada*).
The needle has longitudinal grooves to hold the ink.

Glossary

acharn sak: a tattoo master

abidhamma: the Buddha's teachings

arahat: one who has achieved Nirvana and been liberated from the endless cycle of rebirth

arupaloka: the highest plane of existence

candle ritual: a candle made from hot wax rolled around a wick bound with a *yantra* written on paper or cloth

bhumisparsha mudra: the gesture of enlightenment

bodhisattva: one on the path to Buddhahood

bun phrawees: a thanksgiving festival

caye: a scribe

Chula Sakarat: a lunisolar calendar

cinnabar: mercuric sulphide

deva: a celestial being in the lower heavens

dhamma: the teachings of the Buddha

dharmachakra mudra: a gesture symbolising the Buddha's first sermon

dhyana mudra: a gesture of meditation and tranquillity

dua them: a general term for Tham Lan Na, Tai Khoen and Tai Lue scripts

dukka (Pali):   suffering and its causes

eight time periods: a Tai time counting system used in divination

ekeavisati: a tiger

Gavampati: a legendary scholar

garuda: a Hindu deity depicted as the mount of the Hindu god Vishnu

147

gatha/katha: numbers, letters and symbols read as magical incantations

gradaat saa: mulberry paper used for manuscripts

hamsa: a sacred goose

Hanuman: lord of the monkeys

i cawk: a fork-tailed lizard that brings good luck

ingwet: a magic formula prepared by a shaman

jataka: stories of former lives of the Buddha

karma (*kam*):   the law of cause and effect

kamaloka: the eleven realms of desire

katha (*gatha*):   words of an incantation or spell

khan khru: an altar

kha-tha thon-pis: sacred words to withdraw negative power

kinnara/kinnari: half-human, half-bird

lacquer: made from the resin of the tree *gluta usitata*

leporello: a manuscript that folds in one continuous sheet like a concertina;
    see *pap tup*

life force: a term used to describe units of supernatural power

lik: a script

Maitreya: the Buddha of the future

Mae Phosop: patroness of rice and rice culture

makara: a mythical animal with the head of an elephant and the body of a
    serpent/dragon

mandala: a symbol of *dharmachakra*, the Wheel of Law and endless cycle of
    rebirth

Mara: a demon god

maw paeng: a creator of negative power

metta: loving-kindness, benevolence and harmony

Metta Sutta: a sacred text on the subject of metta

Mount Meru: the sacred five-peaked mountain of Hindu, Jain and
    Buddhist cosmology

Muang/muong: a power centre or sphere of influence, usually a city-state mudra: a gesture

mulberry tree (*Broussonetia papyrifera*):   the inner bark is used for making Shan paper

naga: a mythical sea dragon or serpent associated with water and fertility

Nang Kaew (Nang Kwak):   a female spirit who brings commercial success

Nang Sulat Siwalee (Saraswati):   protector of Buddhist scriptures, education and the arts

Nang Thorani: vanquisher of the demon god Mara

nar: a page of a manuscript

niraya: the lowest plane of existence

numerology: the power of numbers

om: short for the incantation *om mani padme hum*

Pali: Indo-Aryan literary and liturgical language of Theravada Buddhism written in various scripts

Pali incantation: used for healing and good luck

pap kien: a manuscript with folios bound together like a book or flip-chart

pap saa: a mulberry paper manuscript

pap tup: a manuscript in one sheet folded backwards and forwards to create concertina-style pleats; also called *leperello*

paritta: printed texts containing protective words

phaya khaokha: the prince spirit of love

phi lo: a powerful spirit ogre popular in Shan State

Phra Siwali: a magico-religious monk

Phra Upakut: a spirit prince of the underworld who visits earth as a monk

pong pheuw: a space that draws in suffering and unhappiness

porcupine bezoar: a stony secretion which forms in the stomach of a porcupine

positive power: supernatural power that creates good

prasad: a religious/devotiomal building

precepts: Buddhist rules governing behaviour

punnaka: a guardian spirit

rachasee: a king of animals

Rahu: the god of eclipses

ruesi: a hermit

rupaloka: the sixteen realms of form

saiyasart: supernaturalism considered 'not strictly Buddhist'

sangha: monks

saya: an expert in the arts of the supernatural

seub chadaa: coloured ritual flags

Shan: Tai of the Shan States

singha: a mythical lion

sompoy (*Accacia rugata Merr.*):   a local plant used in purification rituals

sud than: a ceremony to draw away evil spirits

Sulat Siwali: Tai form of the Hindu goddess Salasvati

sutta: sacred texts

Tai: people inhabiting Assam, the Shan States, southwest China, Laos and
Thailand who share a common heritage; many subgroups have been
identified.

Tai Yai (also called Shan Proper or Tai Ngio):   Tai of the Shan States and
western Lan Na

thao thang si: guardian spirits

thep: an angel

thien suk lap luk: a good luck incantation

tical: 0.576 ounces (16.33 gm)

Triple Gem: the Buddha, the *sangha* (monks) and the *dhamma* (law)

vihara: main monastery building

yantra: mystical symbolic diagrams and illustrations

Bibliography

Armstrong, Karen. 2001. *Buddha*. UK: Viking Penguin.

Becchetti, Catherine. 1991. *Le mystère dans les lettres: étude sur les yantra bouddhiques du Cambodge et de la Thaïlande*. Bangkok: Editions des cahiers de France.

Berkwitz, Stephen C.; Schober, Juliane; and Brown, Claudia, eds. 2009. *Buddhist Manuscript Cultures: Knowledge, Ritual, and Art*. New York: Routledge.

Brun, Viggo, and Schumacher, Trond. 1994. *Traditional Herbal Medicine in Northern Thailand*. Bangkok: White Lotus.

Bock, Carl. 1884. *Temples and Elephants: Travels in Siam in 1881–1882*; reprint Singapore: Oxford University Press, 1986.

Chen, L.; Wang, X.; and Huang, B. 2015. 'The Genus Hippocampus: A Review on Traditional Medicinal Uses, Chemical Constituents and Pharmacological Properties'. *Journal of Ethnopharmacology* 162: 104–11.

Conway, Susan. 1992. *Thai Textiles*. London: British Museum Press.

—————. 2002. *Silken Threads Lacquer Thrones: Lan Na Court Textiles*. Bangkok: River Books.

—————. 2005. *The Shan: Culture, Art and Craft*s. Bangkok: River Books.

—————. 2007a. 'Shan Buddhism and Culture'. Paper presented at the Conference on Shan Buddhism and Culture, SOAS Centre of Buddhist Studies and the Shan Cultural Association UK, 8 9 December.

—————. 2007b. 'Shan Expressions of Power and Protection'. In *The Secrets of Southeast Asian Textiles: Myth, Status, and the Supernatural*. Bangkok: James H. W. Thompson Foundation and River Books.

—————. 2014. *Tai Magic: Arts of the Supernatural*. Bangkok: River Books.

—————. 2020. *HRH Maha Chakri Sirindhorn's Textile Collection: Symbols of Love and Respect*. Bangkok: Office of HRH Princess Sirindhorn and Amarin Printing and Publishing Public Co., Ltd.

—————. 2024. *Tai Herbalism*. Chiang Mai: Silkworm Books.

Davis, Richard. 1974. 'Tolerance and Intolerance of Ambiguity in Northern Thai Myth and Ritual'. *Ethnology* 13: 1–24.

De Carne, Louis. 1872. *Travels in Indo-China and the Chinese Empire*; reprint Cornell University Library, 2009.

Drouyer, Isabel Azevedo, and Drouyer, René (photographer). 2013. *Thai Magic Tattoos: The Art and Influence of Sak Yant*. Bangkok: River Books.

Eberhardt, Nancy. 2006. *Imagining the Course of Life: Self-Transformation in a Shan Buddhist Community*. Chiang Mai: Silkworm Books.

Geertz, Clifford. 1973. *The Interpretation of Cultures*. New York: Basic Books.

Ginsburg, Henry D. 1989. *Thai Manuscript Painting*. London: British Library.

Grabowsky, Volker, ed. 2022. *Manuscript Cultures and Epigraphy of the Tai World*. Chiang Mai: Silkworm Books.

Grabowsky, Volker, and Turton, Andrew, eds. 2003. *The Gold and Silver Road of Trade and Friendship: The McLeod and Richardson Diplomatic Missions to Tai States in 1837*. Chiang Mai: Silkworm Books.

Green, Colonel Colonel James H., 'The Tribes of Upper Burma North of 24 Degrees Latitude and Their Classification', MA Thesis, University of Cambridge, 1934.

Hall, D. G. E. 1955. *A History of South-East Asia*. London: Macmillan.

Hallet, Holt S. 1890. *A Thousand Miles on an Elephant in the Shan States*. London: William Blackwood and Sons; reprint 1988 White Lotus Co. Ltd Bangkok.

Herbert, Patricia. 2002. 'Burmese Cosmological Manuscripts'. In *Burma: Art and Archaeology*, eds. Alexandra Green and T. Richard Blurton, 77–97. London: British Museum Press.

Hsu, Jeremy, 2017. 'The Hard Truth about the Rhino Horn "Aphrodisiac" Market'. *Scientific American*, 5 April.

Knight, Frank H. 1921. *Risk, Uncertainty and Profit*. Boston: Houghton Mifflin; quoted at the ANRC and RCSD Workshop on 'Human Security and Religious Certainty in Southeast Asia', Chiang Mai, Thailand, 15–17 January 2010.

Kourilsky, Gregory, and Berment, Vincent. 2005. 'Towards a Computerization of the Lao Tham System of Writing'. Paper presented at the First International Conference on Lao Studies, Northern Illinois University, Dekalb, 20–22 May.

Kraisri Nimmanahaeminda. 1967. 'The Lawa Guardian Spirits of Chiangmai'. *Journal of the Siam Society* 55(2): 185–225.

Le May, Reginald. 1926. *An Asian Arcady: The Land and Peoples of Northern Siam*; reprint Bangkok: White Lotus, 1986.

Malinowski, Bronislaw. 1948. *Magic, Science and Religion and Other Essays*. Boston: Beacon Press.

Mayoury and Pheuiphanh Ngaosrivathana. 2009. *The Enduring Sacred Landscape of the Naga*. Chiang Mai: Mekong Press.

McAlister V. 2005. 'Sacred Disease of Our Times: Failure of the Infectious Disease Model of Spongiform Encephalopathy'. *Clinical and Investigative Medicine* 28(3): 101–4.

McDaniel, Justin. 2009. *Gathering Leaves and Lifting Words: Histories of Buddhist Monastic Education in Laos and Thailand*. Chiang Mai: Silkworm Books.

Melchers, K. William. 1910. 'The Thai Invasion of Keng Tung during the Reign of King Rama III'. In Ronald Renard, ed. *Anuson Walter Vella*. Chiang Mai: Mahawitthayalai Phayap. Walter F. Vella Fund and Honolulu, Center for Asian and Pacific Studies, University of Hawaii.

Milne, Leslie, and Cochrane, Wilbur Willis. 1910. *Shans at Home*; reprint New York: Paragon, 1970.

Narujohn Iddhichiracharas. 1980. 'The Northern Thai Peasant Supernaturalism'. In *Buddhism in Northern Thailand*, eds. Saeng Chandrangaam and Narujohn Iddhichiracharas, 100–4. Chiang Mai: The World Fellowship of Buddhists. (Published by Asst. Prof. Saeng Chandrangaam to commemorate the 13th General Conference of the World Fellowship of Buddhists at Chiang Mai, Thailand.)

Nash, J. C. 1966. 'Living with Nats: An Analysis of Animism in Burman Village Social Relations'. In *Anthropological Studies in Theravada Buddhism*, Culture Report Series 13, Southeast Asian Studies, Yale University.

Perdue, Daniel. 2002. *The Course in Buddhist Reasoning and Debate: An Asian Approach to Analytical Thinking Drawn from Indian and Tibetan Sources*. Boston: Shambhala Publications.

Ratanapanna Thera. 1516 CE. *The Jinakalamalipakarana Chronicle* (The Sheaf of Garlands of the Epochs of the Conqueror). Mss Rattvanavihara Temple, Chiang Mai, trans. N. A. Jayawickrama; reprint London: The Pali Text Society Translation Series 36, 1968.

Roos, Anna Marie. 2008. '"Magic Coins" and "Magic Squares": The Discovery of Astrological Sigils in the Oldenburg Letters'. In *Notes and Records of the Royal Society* 62: 271–88.

Sai Kam Mong. 2004. *The History and Development of the Shan Scripts*. Chiang Mai: Silkworm Books.

Saimong Mangrai (Sao), trans. 1981. *The Paedaeng Chronicle and the Jengtung State Chronicle*. Michigan Papers on South and Southeast Asia, No. 19. Ann Arbor: University of Michigan Center for South and Southeast Asian Studies.

San San May. 2011. 'Tattoo Art in Burmese Culture'. Southeast Asia Library Group Newsletter 43, London, December.

Sarassawadee Ongsakul. 2005. *History of La Nan*. Chiang Mai: Silkworm Books.

Scott, J. G., and Hardiman, J. P. 1901. *Gazetteer of Upper Burma and The Shan States*, Pt. II, Vol. II. Rangoon: Superintendent of Government Printing.

Scott, Sir J. George. 1906. *Burma: A Handbook of Practical Information*; reprint Bangkok: Orchid Press, 1999.

Seidenfaden, 1923. 'The Lawa: An Additional Note'. *Journal of the Siam Society* 27(3): 101–2.

Sheravanichkul, Arthid. 2009. 'Pu Khwan Khao Worship of Shan in Yunnan: Fertility and Buddhist Felicity'. *Contemporary Buddhism* 10(1): 159–70.

Shway Yoe (Sir James George Scott). 1882. *The Burman: His Life and Notions*, Vol. I. London: Macmillan; reprint New York: W.W. Norton & Co. Inc., 1963.

Sommai Premchit. *The Lan Na Twelve-month Traditions: An Ethno-historic and Comparative Approach*, Research Report, Faculty of Social Sciences, Chiang Mai University, Thailand, and Centre National de la Recherche Scientifique, France, 1992.

Sommai Premchit and Doré, Amphay. 1974. *L'ecole de la forêt: Un itinéraire spirituel lao*; reprint Aurangabad, India: Kailash Books, 1992.

Sparkes, Stephen. 2005. *Spirits and Souls: Gender and Cosmology in an Isan Village in Northeast Thailand*. Bangkok: White Lotus.

Spiro, Melford E. 1967. *Burmese Supernaturalism: A Study in the Explanation and Reduction of Suffering*. New Jersey: Prentice-Hall.

Tambiah, Stanley Jeyaraja. 1970. *Buddhism and the Spirit Cults in North-east Thailand*. Cambridge: Cambridge University Press.

————. 1976. *World Conqueror and World Renouncer: A Study of Buddhism and Polity in Thailand Against a Historical Background*. Cambridge: Cambridge University Press.

————. 1984. *The Buddhist Saints of the Forest and the Cult of Amulets*. Cambridge: Cambridge University Press.

Tannenbaum, Nicola. 1987. 'Tattoos: Invulnerability and Power in Shan Cosmology'. *American Ethnologist* 14(4): 693–711.

Terweil, B. J. 1994. *Monks and Magic: An Analysis of Religious Ceremonies in Central Thailand*; 3rd reprint Bangkok: White Lotus, 2001.

Vater, Tom, and Aroon Thaewchatturat. 2011. *Sacred Skin: Thailand's Spirit Tattoos*. Bangkok: Visionary World.

Verpoorte, Rob. 2015. 'Food and Medicine: Old Traditions, Novel Opportunities'. *Journal of Ethnopharmacology* 11:29 (editorial).

Wyatt, David K., and Aroonrut Wichienkeeo, trans. 1995. *The Chiang Mai Chronicle*. Chiang Mai: Silkworm Books.

Acknowledgements

Thanks go to the MacArthur Foundation, the British Academy and the James H. W. Thompson Foundation who gave financial support for my research. I would also like to thank Ruth Barnes, who by showing me some spirit cloths in the Ashmolean Museum, Oxford, planted the idea for this project. Thanks also go to the late Henry Ginsburg, Jana Igunma and San San May from the British Library, and Fiona Kerlogue of the Horniman Museum. In the United States, thanks go to Allen Thrasher and Lien-Huong Fiedler from the Asia Department, The Library of Congress, Washington DC, and Mattiebelle Gittinger from the Textile Museum, Washington DC.

I would like to acknowledge friends and colleagues in Thailand and Myanmar. They include Kam Indra and Suriya Smutkupt of Chiang Mai University; Phra Payongsak of Wat Pa Daed, Chiang Mai; Phra Jeruwana Yeenoon and Phra Supachai Chayasupho of Wat Suan Dork, Chiang Mai; and Phra Warinda of Wat Tiyasathan, Mae Daeng. I would also like to thank Panpen Kruathai, Srilao Ketphrom and Amornrath Feungworatham from the Social Research Institute, Chiang Mai University, and Wiluck Sripasang and Tonapha Pusadee from Chiang Mai University. The *saya* Sai Da and spirit medium Nang Lord were extremely helpful. Louis Gabaude and individual members of the Informal Northern Thai Group gave additional data on Tai supernaturalism.

Akadej Nakbunlang, Paothong Thongchua, Sirot Chutiwat and Anusak Parnichyakorn allowed me to take photographs of their collections. Other collectors in Chiang Mai who contributed chose to remain anonymous.

I would also like to acknowledge the Buddhist communities who allowed access to their repositories, especially their manuscripts.

In Chiang Rai, I am indebted to the Ven. Phrakhru Vimol Silpakit of Mahachulalongkornrajavidyalaya University, Wat Phra Kaew; Rebecca Weldon Sithiwong, consultant to Wat Phra Kaew; the Rai Mae Fah Luang Museum and Supachai Sittilert of the Hong Luang Saeng Kaew Museum. I would also like to thank the monks of Wat Pang Mu in Mae Hong Son; also in Mae Hong Son Khun Yai Yotmanee, Khun Gaysorn and Khun Kan-na (Sua Yen) Rubnamtham. Lung Ae Piya Wong, Acharn Baan Langkhu and Khun Long Tan Kyo Ho provided information on the practices of lay *saya*. I am grateful to Khun Tun Yee who translated into English some supernatural prescriptions interpreted by Long Te Za who is Shan, and Long Noi Na who is Tai Yuan.

In the Shan States, I would like to thank Nang Voe Pat who accompanied me on several research trips. Thanks also go to Lung Saw Jing, the lay *saya* Maha Kaew and Phra Sai Khemacari from Wat Chieng Yin, Keng Tung; Phraku Wasan from Wat Ho Khong, Keng Tung; and librarian Phra Sitilong and the monks of Wat In who were also extremely helpful. I am appreciative of the vision provided by my publisher Trasvin Jittidercharak and by Phra Dhammasami from Shan State Buddhist University.

Finally, I wish to thank my friend and colleague Dr Gary Suwannarat who has spent her working life in Southeast Asia and is familiar with many aspects of Tai culture. She has always given generously of her time and knowledge and accompanied me on some field trips.